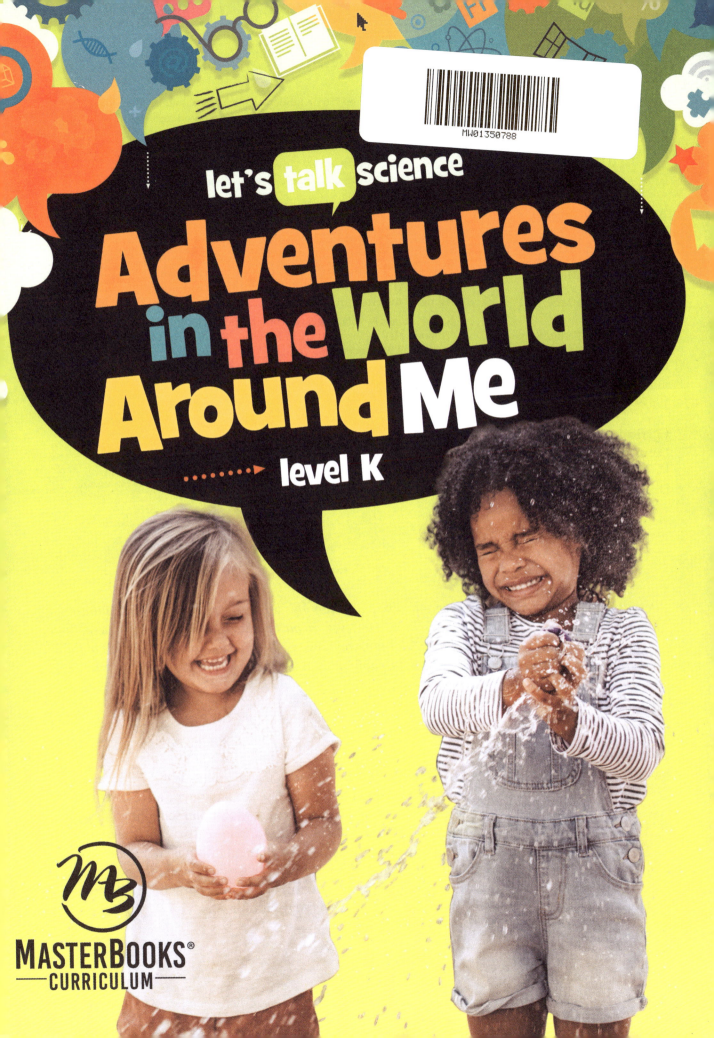

Author: Carrie Linquist

Master Books Creative Team:

Editor: Willow Meek

Design: Terry White

Cover Design: Diana Bogardus

Copy Editors:
Judy Lewis
Willow Meek

Curriculum Review:
Laura Welch
Kristen Pratt
Diana Bogardus

First printing: August 2021

Copyright © 2021 by Carrie Lindquist and Master Books®. All rights reserved. No part of this book may be used or reproduced in any manner whatsoever without written permission of the publisher, except in the case of brief quotations in articles and reviews. For information write:

Master Books®, P.O. Box 726, Green Forest, AR 72638
Master Books® is a division of the New Leaf Publishing Group, Inc.

ISBN: 978-1-68344-265-3
ISBN: 978-1-61458-786-6 (digital)

Unless otherwise noted, Scripture taken from the Holy Bible, NEW INTERNATIONAL READER'S VERSION®. Copyright © 1996, 1998 Biblica. All rights reserved throughout the world. Used by permission of Biblica.

Scriptures marked (NIV) taken from the Holy Bible, New International Version®, NIV®. Copyright © 1973, 1978, 1984, 2011 by Biblica, Inc.™ Used by permission of Zondervan. All rights reserved worldwide.

All images are shutterstock.com.

Printed in the United States of America.

Please visit our website for other great titles: www.masterbooks.com

Permission is granted for copies of reproducible pages from this text to be made for use with immediate family members living in the same household. However, no part of this book may be reproduced, copied, broadcast, stored, or shared in any form beyond this use. Permission for any other use of the material must be requested by email from the publisher at info@nlpg.com.

About the Author

Carrie Lindquist is a homeschool graduate, wife to Wayne, and momma to two energetic boys. She is a passionate advocate for homeschooling and loves helping new-to-homeschooling moms to realize that homeschooling through the early years isn't scary — it's really just an extension of all the fun things they are already doing with their children! When she isn't cleaning the endless little messes her boys create, you can find her encouraging moms to embrace the calling of everyday faithfulness.

Table of Contents

- **Course Objectives** 4
- **A Note from the Author** 4
- **Course Components** 5
- **Master Materials List** 6
- **Schedule** 9
- **Junior Science Certificate** 167

Page	Topic
13	All About Me
17	Things I Can Taste
21	Things I Can Hear
25	Things I Can Feel
29	Things I Can Smell
33	Things I Can See
37	Taking Care of Me 1
41	Taking Care of Me 2
45	Tools We Use in Science
49	Light and Shadows
53	Primary and Secondary Colors
57	Size
61	Shape
65	Exploring My World
69	Water
73	Heat
77	Living and Non-Living
81	Plants
87	Trees
91	Birds
95	Fish
99	Sharks
103	Whales and Dolphins
107	Animals
113	Reptiles
119	Habitats
125	Caring for the World Around Us
129	The Weather
133	Spring & Summer
137	Fall & Winter
141	Daytime
145	Nighttime
151	Rocks & Minerals
155	Fossils
159	Dinosaurs
163	Conclusion

Course Description

Approximately 20 minutes per lesson, two times per week

Designed for kindergarten in a one-year course

Let's Talk Science: Adventures in the World Around Me introduces young learners to the amazing world of science. Through interactive lessons, hands-on activities, crafts, and engaging worksheets, students will discover God as the Creator of the world around them.

As they explore God's creation, students will discover how to use their five senses to investigate the world around them, learn basic properties of physical science, explore living and non-living things, and develop a love for learning more about God's creation through science.

Course Objectives

Students completing this course will:

- Learn that God is the Creator.

- Discover how they can use their five senses to learn more about the world around them.

- Develop their curiosity and build a foundation for future scientific study.

- Explore the tools we use in science, light and shadows, colors, size, shape, water, heat, living things, habitats, how to care for God's creation, weather, seasons, day and night, rocks, minerals, fossils, and dinosaurs.

- Enjoy learning about science through hands-on activities and crafts.

A note from the author

Welcome to *Let's Talk Science: Adventures in the World Around Me*! I'm so excited for you and your child to begin this adventure together. This stage of learning is so much fun and often filled with wide-eyed wonder as your child begins to discover more of the world around them.

If your child is anything like my children, your days are likely filled with many, many questions about the world they see around them. Each question sparked by curiosity becomes an amazing opportunity to learn, discover, and explore God's creation together. This course is inspired by the questions my sons have asked and the adventures we've had as we've answered those questions together.

Let's Talk Science: Adventures in the World Around Me is designed to be a lot of fun, interactive, hands-on, and easy to prepare for. This course is also designed to encourage curiosity — and if your child is particularly interested in a topic or question, I invite you to spend some time exploring God's world together through books, videos, and resources. Make this course your own, and have fun!

It is my prayer that as your child completes this course, they discover God as the Creator and develop a lifelong love for exploring His creation through science.

Course Components

- "The Adventures of Gideon and Mr. Snuggly" introduce the science topic for the week in a short story. These stories are designed to develop the student's imagination and curiosity.

- Engaging worksheets encourage your student's creativity and critical thinking skills.

- Most of the weekly lessons feature a hands-on activity or craft to reinforce the week's topic. The activities are designed to be easy to prepare for, and most require materials you may already have on hand.

- A Master Materials List provides an at-a-glance view of the materials your student will need to complete activities during each week.

- This course is designed to be interactive. Be sure to take time to pause after questions in the text and explore the topic with your student. Encourage their curiosity and questions — you may both be able to learn something new together!

Master Materials List

Week 2
- [ ] Mirror

Week 4
- [ ] Something cold, like an ice cube or popsicle
- [ ] Something warm, like a cup of tea or hot chocolate
- [ ] Something cool, like cool water from the sink or food from the refrigerator

Week 5
- [ ] Pencil
- [ ] A few fragrant food items such as sliced orange, cheese crackers, vanilla, flavored cereal, garlic, onion, etc.
- [ ] Cup or container for each food selected
- [ ] Blindfold

Week 6
- [ ] Mirror

Week 7
- [ ] Fine glitter
- [ ] Plate
- [ ] Hand towel
- [ ] Sink
- [ ] Hand soap

Week 8
- [ ] A band-aid
- [ ] Sink
- [ ] Clean towel or cotton pad
- [ ] Optional: mild soap

Week 9
- [ ] An apple
- [ ] Cutting board
- [ ] Knife (adult only)
- [ ] Magnifying glass
- [ ] Ruler

Week 10
- [ ] Flashlight
- [ ] Opaque object such as a book or stuffed animal

Week 11
- [ ] 6 cotton swabs
- [ ] Washable red, blue, and yellow paint
- [ ] Paper
- [ ] Plastic tablecloth

Week 12
- [ ] An assortment of objects that are of small, medium, and large sizes

Week 14
- [ ] A flower
- [ ] Ruler
- [ ] Magnifying glass

Week 15
- [ ] Pitcher or container of water
- [ ] Clear glass cup
- [ ] Water
- [ ] Coffee maker or tea kettle
- [ ] Coffee mug
- [ ] Ice cubes

Week 16
- [ ] Your favorite cookie recipe
- [ ] Ingredients and supplies for recipe

Week 17
- [ ] Stuffed animal, baby doll, or action figure

Week 18
- [ ] Glue stick
- [ ] Construction paper
- [ ] Packet of seeds (flowers, herbs, etc.)
- [ ] Potting soil
- [ ] Small pot

Week 20
- [ ] Construction paper
- [ ] Scissors
- [ ] Googly eyes
- [ ] Glue
- [ ] Craft feathers
- [ ] 2 paper plates
- [ ] Stapler
- [ ] Crayons or markers
- [ ] Hole punch
- [ ] Yarn

Week 21
- [ ] Construction paper
- [ ] Glue stick
- [ ] Pencil
- [ ] Scissors
- [ ] Googly eye
- [ ] Popsicle stick
- [ ] Optional: glitter glue or craft gems

Week 22
- [ ] Glue
- [ ] Clothespin

Week 23
- [ ] Ziploc® sandwich bag
- [ ] Large bowl filled with ice water
- [ ] ½ to 1 cup butter or shortening
- [ ] Dish soap

Week 25
- [ ] Paint
- [ ] Paintbrush
- [ ] Paper plate
- [ ] Glue
- [ ] Scissors

Week 26
- [ ] Glue stick
- [ ] Scissors

Week 28
- [ ] Blue construction paper
- [ ] Crayons
- [ ] Cotton balls
- [ ] Glue
- [ ] Blue paint
- [ ] Cotton swab
- [ ] Tablecloth

Week 29
- [ ] Paper plate
- [ ] Yellow or orange paint
- [ ] Paintbrush
- [ ] Scissors
- [ ] Yellow or orange construction paper
- [ ] Tablecloth

Week 30
- ☐ White, blue, black, and orange construction paper
- ☐ Pencil
- ☐ Yarn
- ☐ Scissors
- ☐ Glue stick
- ☐ Googly eyes
- ☐ Optional: cotton balls or white glitter glue

Week 31
- ☐ Globe or ball
- ☐ Flashlight
- ☐ Dark room

Week 32
- ☐ Black construction paper
- ☐ Pencil
- ☐ Gray paint
- ☐ Paper plate
- ☐ Tinfoil
- ☐ White or silver glitter glue
- ☐ Tablecloth
- ☐ Scissors
- ☐ Brad fasteners

Week 33
- ☐ A pumice stone
- ☐ Magnifying glass
- ☐ Salt

Week 34
- ☐ Plate
- ☐ Chocolate chip cookie
- ☐ Toothpick or chopstick
- ☐ Paintbrush

Week 35
- ☐ Play-Doh®

First Quarter Schedule

Date	Day	Assignment	Due Date	✓
Week 1	Day	Read and complete Day 1 • All About Me • Pages 13–14		
	Day	Read and complete Day 2 • All About Me • Pages 15–16		
Week 2	Day	Read and complete Day 1 • Things I Can Taste • Pages 17–19		
	Day	Read and complete Day 2 • Things I Can Taste • Page 20		
Week 3	Day	Read and complete Day 1 • Things I Can Hear • Pages 21–22		
	Day	Read and complete Day 2 • Things I Can Hear • Pages 23–24		
Week 4	Day	Read and complete Day 1 • Things I Can Feel • Pages 25–26		
	Day	Read and complete Day 2 • Things I Can Feel • Pages 27–28		
Week 5	Day	Read and complete Day 1 • Things I Can Smell • Pages 29–30		
	Day	Read and complete Day 2 • Things I Can Smell • Pages 31–32		
Week 6	Day	Read and complete Day 1 • Things I Can See • Pages 33–34		
	Day	Read and complete Day 2 • Things I Can See • Pages 35–36		
Week 7	Day	Read and complete Day 1 • Taking Care of Me 1 • Pages 37–38		
	Day	Read and complete Day 2 • Taking Care of Me 1 • Pages 39–40		
Week 8	Day	Read and complete Day 1 • Taking Care of Me 2 • Pages 41–42		
	Day	Read and complete Day 2 • Taking Care of Me 2 • Pages 43–44		
Week 9	Day	Read and complete Day 1 • Tools We Use in Science • Pages 45–46		
	Day	Read and complete Day 2 • Tools We Use in Science • Pages 47–48		

Adventures in the World Around Me ········▶ Schedule

Second Quarter Schedule

Date	Day	Assignment	Due Date	✓
Week 10	Day	Read and complete Day 1 • Light and Shadows • Pages 49–50		
	Day	Read and complete Day 2 • Light and Shadows • Pages 51–52		
Week 11	Day	Read and complete Day 1 • Primary and Secondary Colors Pages 53–54		
	Day	Read and complete Day 2 • Primary and Secondary Colors Pages 55–56		
Week 12	Day	Read and complete Day 1 • Size • Pages 57–58		
	Day	Read and complete Day 2 • Size • Pages 59–60		
Week 13	Day	Read and complete Day 1 • Shape • Pages 61–62		
	Day	Read and complete Day 2 • Shape • Pages 63–64		
Week 14	Day	Read and complete Day 1 • Exploring My World • Pages 65–67		
	Day	Read and complete Day 2 • Exploring My World • Page 68		
Week 15	Day	Read and complete Day 1 • Water • Pages 69–70		
	Day	Read and complete Day 2 • Water • Pages 71–72		
Week 16	Day	Read and complete Day 1 • Heat • Pages 73–74		
	Day	Read and complete Day 2 • Heat • Pages 75–76		
Week 17	Day	Read and complete Day 1 • Living and Non-Living • Pages 77–78		
	Day	Read and complete Day 2 • Living and Non-Living • Pages 79–80		
Week 18	Day	Read and complete Day 1 • Plants • Pages 81–83		
	Day	Read and complete Day 2 • Plants • Pages 85–86		

Third Quarter Schedule

Date	Day	Assignment	Due Date	✓
Week 19	Day	Read and complete Day 1 • Trees • Pages 87–88		
	Day	Read and complete Day 2 • Trees • Pages 89–90		
Week 20	Day	Read and complete Day 1 • Birds • Pages 91–93		
	Day	Read and complete Day 2 • Birds • Page 94		
Week 21	Day	Read and complete Day 1 • Fish • Pages 95–96		
	Day	Read and complete Day 2 • Fish • Pages 97–98		
Week 22	Day	Read and complete Day 1 • Sharks • Pages 99–100		
	Day	Read and complete Day 2 • Sharks • Pages 101–102		
Week 23	Day	Read and complete Day 1 • Whales and Dolphins • Pages 103–104		
	Day	Read and complete Day 2 • Whales and Dolphins • Pages 105–106		
Week 24	Day	Read and complete Day 1 • Animals • Pages 107–109		
	Day	Read and complete Day 2 • Animals • Pages 110–112		
Week 25	Day	Read and complete Day 1 • Reptiles • Pages 113–115		
	Day	Read and complete Day 2 • Reptiles • Pages 117–118		
Week 26	Day	Read and complete Day 1 • Habitats • Pages 119–120		
	Day	Read and complete Day 2 • Habitats • Pages 121–123		
Week 27	Day	Read and complete Day 1 • Caring for the World Around Us Pages 125–126		
	Day	Read and complete Day 2 • Caring for the World Around Us Pages 127–128		

Fourth Quarter Schedule

Date	Day	Assignment	Due Date	✓
Week 28	Day 1	Read and complete Day 1 • The Weather • Pages 129–130		
	Day 2	Read and complete Day 2 • The Weather • Pages 131–132		
Week 29	Day 1	Read and complete Day 1 • Spring & Summer • Pages 133–134		
	Day 2	Read and complete Day 2 • Spring & Summer • Pages 135–136		
Week 30	Day 1	Read and complete Day 1 • Fall & Winter • Pages 137–138		
	Day 2	Read and complete Day 2 • Fall & Winter • Pages 139–140		
Week 31	Day 1	Read and complete Day 1 • Daytime • Pages 141–142		
	Day 2	Read and complete Day 2 • Daytime • Pages 143–144		
Week 32	Day 1	Read and complete Day 1 • Nighttime • Pages 145–147		
	Day 2	Read and complete Day 2 • Nighttime • Pages 148–149		
Week 33	Day 1	Read and complete Day 1 • Rocks & Minerals • Pages 151–152		
	Day 2	Read and complete Day 2 • Rocks & Minerals • Pages 153–154		
Week 34	Day 1	Read and complete Day 1 • Fossils • Pages 155–157		
	Day 2	Read and complete Day 2 • Fossils • Page 158		
Week 35	Day 1	Read and complete Day 1 • Dinosaurs • Pages 159–160		
	Day 2	Read and complete Day 2 • Dinosaurs • Pages 161–162		
Week 36	Day 1	Read and complete Day 1 • Conclusion • Pages 163–164		
	Day 2	Read and complete Day 2 • Conclusion • Page 165		

All About Me

week 1

Day 1

The Adventures of Gideon and Mr. Snuggly

Hello, friend! My name is Gideon, and this is my teddy bear, Mr. Snuggly. Mr. Snuggly has been my favorite teddy bear ever since I was a baby. I'm a lot bigger now, but he still comes with me everywhere I go. We go on a lot of adventures together! I'm getting ready to start a new adventure: exploring the world God made around me. Would you like to join the adventure?

When I grow up, I want to be a scientist. A scientist explores the world God made. Scientists can study things like rocks, animals, the ocean, the sun, moon, stars, machines, and so much more. There is a lot we can learn together; let's get started!

Welcome to our science adventure! We're going to explore the world around us, and we will have a lot of fun together. Let's begin by learning more about you!

Scientists ask many questions to help them learn about the world around them. As we begin our adventure, my first question is: Who made you? When we have a question, we can look in the Bible for an answer. The Bible is God's Word to us.

Let's read Psalm 139:13–14 from the Bible. As I read, remember that when these verses say "you," they are talking about God. Ready? See if you can hear the answer to the question, "Who made you?" as I read:

You created the deepest parts of my being. You put me together inside my mother's body. How you made me is amazing and wonderful. I praise you for that. What you have done is wonderful. I know that very well.

Did you hear the answer? Who made you? God made you!

God gave you the color of your eyes and hair, the shape of your nose and ears, your smile, your giggle, and everything that makes you, you. God made you unique, there isn't anyone else just like you. Let's look at the way God made you unique today.

Teacher tip: You may write the answers and have the student trace them with a pencil or highlighter if the student isn't writing well at this stage.

All about you! Write the answers. Then use a crayon to color the box in with your eye and hair color.

My name is: _____

I am _____ years old.

My eyes are this color: ☐

My hair is this color: ☐

Adventures in the World Around Me ……▶ Week 1

Day

In our last lesson, we learned that God created you. Did you know that God also knows you? In Psalm 139:1–4, it says,

Lord, you have seen what is in my heart. You know all about me. You know when I sit down and when I get up. You know what I'm thinking even though you are far away. You know when I go out to work and when I come back home. You know exactly how I live. Lord, even before I speak a word, you know all about it.

Isn't that amazing? God created you, and He knows all about you. God made you unique for a special purpose, to bring Him glory and praise. God gave you special talents and interests. When you follow God, He can use your special talents and interests to show the people around you more about Him. Maybe you love to sing, or color, or tell jokes that make people laugh. What is one of your special talents?

Teacher tip: If your student can't think of a special talent themselves, point out something they are good at. Talk about ways they can use their talent in the future.

God created each of us with different special talents and things we like to do. God can use our abilities in lots of different jobs. What kind of job do you think you would like to have when you grow up?

Teacher tip: If your student is uncertain, you can discuss different jobs they may be good at. You can also share what you wanted to be as a child, what you are now, and how God has used you in that position.

name

Draw a picture of what you would like to be when you grow up.

Things I Can Taste

week 2

Day 1

The Adventures of Gideon and Mr. Snuggly

Oh, hello there, friend! I just finished eating my lunch. I had a grilled cheese sandwich. The creamy cheese in the middle of the toasted bread was a little salty — but it was delicious! I was still hungry afterward, so Mom gave me some sweet, juicy grapes to eat as well.

I'm about to go to the park now with Mr. Snuggly and Mom. When we get home, we'll have a salty, sour pickle and sweet, crunchy carrots for a snack. I love to eat all different kinds of food. Hmm, that makes me wonder, how are we able to taste food? Let's explore our sense of taste today!

God gave us our sense of taste. What is your favorite thing to taste?

Teacher tip: Allow student to answer. You may also share your favorite taste.

We taste food through our tongue. Look in the mirror and stick out your tongue. Can you see all of the little bumps on your tongue? Those special bumps are called papillae (said this way: pŭh-pĭl-ē). We have more to learn, but before we go any further, we need to wash our hands.

Teacher tip: Help your student wash their hands then return to the mirror.

Mirror ✓

Weekly materials list

Adventures in the World Around Me — Week 2

17

Look into the mirror and stick your tongue out again. Feel the top of your tongue with your finger. Can you feel the bumpy papillae under your finger? The bumpy, rough papillae help your tongue move food around in your mouth as you chew it — but that's not the only job of your papillae!

Many of the papillae on your tongue also hold your taste buds. Your taste buds are what allow you to taste different flavors like sweet, bitter, salty, and sour. Our taste buds help us enjoy many different types of food. We can enjoy the taste of a sweet watermelon slice all by itself. Or we can enjoy many flavors together in a spicy salsa.

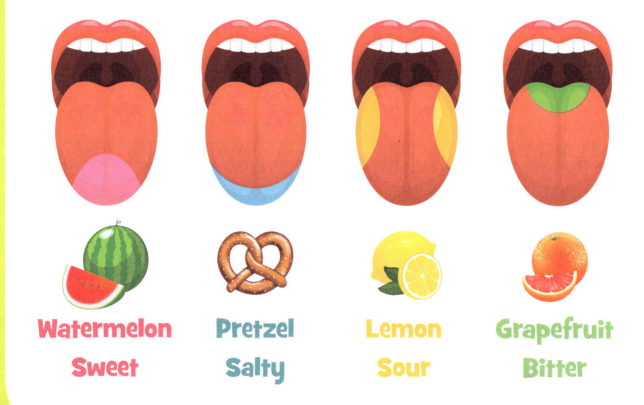

Watermelon — Sweet

Pretzel — Salty

Lemon — Sour

Grapefruit — Bitter

name

Match each food to the word that describes how it tastes.

Sweet

Salty

Sour

Bitter

Day

We're learning about our sense of taste. We can use our tongue to help us taste many different flavors. We can look in the kitchen to see if we can find a sweet, salty, sour, and bitter taste. Once we find one of the flavors, let's taste it together! Ready to have fun?

Activity directions:

1. Go into the kitchen with your student.

materials needed
☐ Tastable items in the kitchen

The first flavor we need to find is sweet. Can you think of something that would be sweet?

2. If you have the item the student named, you can taste it. If you do not, see what else you can find such as fruit, maple syrup, cookies, or a pinch of sugar. Once you've each tasted the item, describe it to each other.

Do you like the flavor?

The next flavor we need to find is salty. Can you think of something that would be salty?

3. Repeat step two with the salty item. Sample salty ideas: salted chips, cheese crackers, pretzels, pinch of salt.

The next flavor we need to find is sour. Can you think of something that would be sour?

4. Repeat step two with the sour item. Sample sour ideas: lemon juice, vinegar, pickles.

The last flavor we need to find is bitter. Can you think of something that would be bitter?

5. Repeat step two with the bitter item. Sample bitter ideas: cup of black coffee, grapefruit, dark chocolate, unsweetened cocoa powder.

We taste sweet, salty, bitter, and sour flavors. Do you smile when you taste something sweet? Or scrunch up your face when taking a sour bite? Draw a picture of what your face looks like when tasting different flavors!

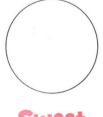
Sweet

Salty

Sour

Bitter

Things I Can Hear

week 3

Day 1

The Adventures of Gideon and Mr. Snuggly

I'm glad you're back! I was listening to music with Mr. Snuggly right before you came today. Do you like to listen to music? My favorite music has Bible verses in the song. As I learn how to sing the song, I also get to memorize a Bible verse!

Music isn't the only thing I like to listen to, though. I also like to listen to the birds singing outside, my dad playing his guitar, and my cat purring. That gives me an idea! Have you ever wondered how we can hear all kinds of different things? Let's explore our sense of hearing today!

Our ears allow us to hear many different sounds. Through our ears, we can hear loud noises like a dog barking, or quiet noises like a whisper. Can you think of a loud noise you've heard?

Teacher tip: Allow student to answer.

What about a quiet noise you've heard?

Teacher tip: Allow student to answer.

Do you see the hole near the bottom of my ear? This leads to the ear canal, which carries sound to the second part of the ear: the middle ear. There is a special part inside the middle ear called the eardrum. The sounds around you cause the eardrum to move. Its movement causes three very tiny bones to vibrate.

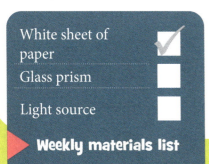

- ☑ White sheet of paper
- ☐ Glass prism
- ☐ Light source

▶ **Weekly materials list**

When the bones vibrate, the vibrations travel through to the inner ear. The inner ear then helps those vibrations move to your brain. Your brain is inside of your head. Your brain helps you think, speak, move, and much more. Your brain uses the vibrations to tell you what you're hearing. Did you know that so many parts are working together to help you hear every sound around you? What an amazing design God created!

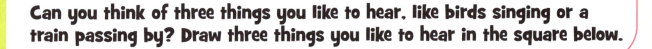

Can you think of three things you like to hear, like birds singing or a train passing by? Draw three things you like to hear in the square below.

Day

In the Bible, we learn that God created a perfect world. But, His creation was broken by sin, and things are no longer perfect. Sometimes, that means our bodies don't work quite the way they were designed to. When this happens, a person may have a very hard time hearing things. Or they may not be able to hear anything at all.

Teacher tip: If your student is unfamiliar with creation and the Fall, you can spend time together as a family reading Genesis chapters 1–3.

Do you remember when we talked about how God gave us each special talents and abilities? God gave people the ability to be creative and to solve problems. People used their talents and abilities to find ways to help people who cannot hear.

One way people found a way to help is through hearing aids. When it is hard for a person to hear, they can use a hearing aid. The hearing aid may sit in or around a person's ear and it helps them to hear the sounds around them. I'm glad God gave people wisdom so that they could create hearing aids!

Hearing aids aren't always able to help, though. When a person cannot hear anything, they are not able to hear us talk to them. To help, people created a way to speak with their hands so that we can all communicate. We call it sign language. Through sign language, we can use our hands and motions to talk with someone who cannot hear our voices.

Let's learn some sign language together!

Adventures in the World Around Me ......▶ Week 3

Activity directions:

1. Sing the alphabet song with your student.

Did you know we can also use our hands to sing the alphabet? Let's practice the American Sign Language alphabet together.

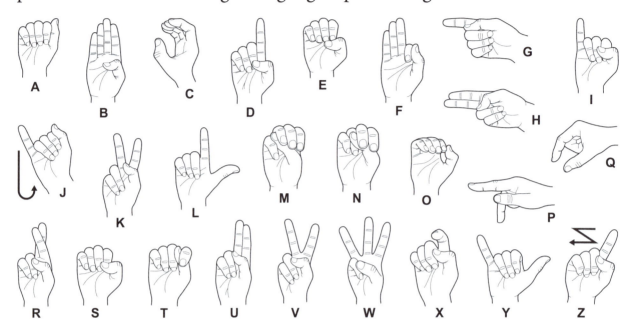

2. Practice making each letter shown below with your student.

3. Sing the alphabet song again, while making the letters with your hand.

4. Optional: Help your student spell their name in sign language.

We can also use our hands to communicate different words to each other. Let's practice a few words in sign language!

5. Pick one or several words from below to learn in sign language. See if you can use these signs to communicate with each other throughout the day.

Yes **No** **Hello** **Goodbye** **Please**

Things I Can Feel

week 4

Day

The Adventures of Gideon and Mr. Snuggly

Hi there! I just finished washing my hands with slippery soap and warm water. After my hands were washed, I dried them on a soft towel. Isn't it fun to feel different things?

Once, I was playing with Mr. Snuggly and got into some trouble because I found a container of birdseed. I opened the container and put my hands inside; the seeds felt so bumpy and silly in my hands! I grabbed a handful of the seeds and let them slip through my fingers to the floor. I learned a good lesson that day — be careful what you touch! I had to help my mom clean up the big mess I made; it wasn't an easy job.

I can feel many different things with my hands. Do you ever wonder how we can feel things? Let's explore our sense of touch today!

God created us with the ability to feel all kinds of different things through our skin. Underneath the surface of our skin, hundreds and thousands of nerves travel through our bodies. Our nerves carry messages through our body and to our brain. Our brain uses those messages to help us understand what we are feeling.

Nerves help us to be able to feel many different textures and temperatures. We use the nerves in our hands and fingertips to feel things throughout the day like warm water, cold ice cubes, hard blocks, and soft blankets. What is something you like to feel in your hands?

Teacher tip: Allow student to answer.

We can feel things that are hard, soft, smooth, rough, or sticky. Let's go on a touch scavenger hunt together to find something that feels hard, soft, smooth, rough, or sticky! (A scavenger hunt is when we go search for a list of things.)

Can you find one object in our house that is hard, one that is soft, one that is smooth, and one that is rough? I'll help! Once we find an object, you can draw it in the box below.

Hard

Soft

Smooth

Rough

Adventures in the World Around Me ······▶ Week 4

Day

name

Our touch scavenger hunt sure was fun! Our sense of touch helps us feel things we enjoy like a loving hug, a fuzzy puppy, a warm cup of hot cocoa, a soft blanket, or even a cold popsicle.

Did you know that God also gave us our sense of touch to help keep us safe? For example, what happens if your hand accidentally touches something that is too hot or too cold for you?

Teacher tip: Allow student to answer.

When your hand touches something that is too hot or too cold, your hand quickly pulls away from that object. God designed your body to pull away from something too hot or too cold before you can even think about it! That helps to keep your skin safe from a temperature that could hurt it.

Our hands and body can feel things that are cool, cold, warm, or hot. Let's have some fun feeling something cool, cold, and warm today!

materials needed

- [ ] Something cold, like an ice cube or popsicle
- [ ] Something warm, like a cup of tea or hot chocolate
- [ ] Something cool, like cool water from the sink or food from the refrigerator

Activity directions:

1. Place the cold, cool, and warm items on the table in front of your student.
2. Instruct your student to touch or eat the cool item (if edible).

What does it feel like? Does it feel comfortable to touch?

3. Instruct your student to touch or eat the cold item (if edible).

What does it feel like? Does it feel comfortable to touch?

4. Instruct your student to touch or eat the warm item (if edible).

What does it feel like? Does it feel comfortable to touch?

There are also many hot objects in our house. We must be careful not to touch things that are hot because they can burn us. Can you think of something that is hot?

5. Discuss things in the house that are too hot to touch, such as the stove.

Be careful not to touch these things.

Draw a line to match each object with the way it feels.

Hot

Soft

Cold

Rough

Things I Can Smell

week 5

Day

The Adventures of Gideon and Mr. Snuggly

Oh, hello friend! Our house smells a little stinky today because there was a skunk in our yard last night. When a skunk is scared or threatened by something, it can spray a very stinky liquid. The disgusting smell creates a distraction so that the skunk can run away to safety. Last night, our puppy accidentally scared the skunk in our yard! The skunk sprayed our puppy and then it ran away — pee-yew!

We've given our puppy a lot of baths today to wash away the strong smell that the skunk sprayed. Hopefully, our puppy will smell good again soon! We can smell many different things like pretty flowers, freshly baked cookies, yummy peaches, and even skunks. Some things smell good and other things smell bad. Have you ever wondered how we can smell different things? Let's learn more about our sense of smell!

God created us with the ability to smell all kinds of different things. What is your favorite smell?

Teacher tip: Allow student to answer. You may also share your favorite smell.

We use our noses to smell. Take a deep breath in — as you breathe in, your nose gathers information from the air around you. Special receptors (cells that receive smells) inside your nose then send the information to your brain so that you can smell a fresh flower, watermelon bath soap, pizza, oranges, and so much more!

God designed us to be able to smell four basic types of smells. We can smell things that are fresh, like sweet oranges. Spicy is the second type of smell — you might smell a spicy scent from hot peppers or spicy salsa.

The third type of smell is putrid — this type doesn't smell good! Things like skunk spray and rotting food smell putrid. Putrid scents may make you want to plug your nose! The fourth type of scent is called fragrant. Flowers and fresh peaches are examples of beautiful, fragrant smells.

Use a blue crayon to circle the items that smell good to you.

Day

name _____

Teacher tip: Prepare food items ahead of time — but don't let your student see what you've chosen before the lesson.

Did you know that your sense of taste and smell work together to help you fully enjoy the food you eat? God designed us to be able to enjoy both the taste and smell of food. Sometimes when we are sick with a stuffy nose, we are not able to smell very well. When this happens, we're not able to taste food as well either. God created our bodies with many parts that work together!

Our sense of smell helps us decide if something is good and safe or if it is not good and unsafe. For example, if I slice a fresh peach, your sense of smell would help you know the fruit is ripe and ready to eat. But when you open the lid to a stinky garbage can, your sense of smell lets you know to stay away.

You smell many things throughout the day. Your brain helps you recognize different smells. Some smells, like freshly baked cookies, may make you feel happy. It may even remind you of a time you helped to make cookies! Your brain helps you to remember what different smells are, or what the smell might mean. Let's do an activity to see what smells you can recognize!

materials needed
- [ ] A few fragrant food items such as sliced orange, cheese crackers, vanilla, flavored cereal, garlic, onion, etc.
- [ ] Cup or container for each food selected
- [ ] Blindfold

Activity directions:

1. If your student is comfortable, use the blindfold to cover their eyes or have them keep their eyes closed.
2. Give your student the first container with a fragrant piece of food.

Smell the container and describe what you're smelling. Does it smell good or bad?

Adventures in the World Around Me ······▶ Week 5

Can you guess what you smelled? Now look in the container to see if you were right.

3. Repeat until the student has smelled each item. Remove the blindfold or have the student open their eyes.

Do you like to smell freshly baked cookies, flowers, or a yummy dinner? Draw your favorite thing to smell below.

Things I Can See

week 6

Day 1

The Adventures of Gideon and Mr. Snuggly

I'm glad you're here, friend! Yesterday afternoon there was a big storm. It rained so hard! As the storm began to go away, I looked out the window and saw the most beautiful rainbow. It spread across the sky, and I saw red, orange, yellow, green, blue, indigo, and violet all in a row. It was beautiful!

I use my eyes to see things all throughout the day. Today I saw my mom brush my big sister's hair. I also looked closely at the strawberries in my cereal — I counted as many of the small seeds as I could. I use my eyes as I draw and color, and also as I run and play. Would you like to explore our sense of sight today? Let's get started!

God created people with eyes. Our eyes help us to see the world around us. Look into my eyes. What do you see?

Teacher tip: Allow student to examine your eyes. They may mention the eyebrows or lashes, pupil, or the color of your eyes.

Now look at your eyes in the mirror. Do you see the colored part of your eye? The colored part of the eye is called the iris. If you look closely, you may see a beautiful design in the iris! People can have different colored irises. What color is your iris? Do you and I have the same or different colored irises?

Mirror ✓

▶ Weekly materials list

Teacher tip: Allow student to answer. You can also ask the student to compare iris colors with other members of the family.

Look at your iris in the mirror again. What color do you see? Choose a crayon or marker that is closest to the color of your iris then color the eyes below to match your eyes.

name _____

materials needed
☐ Mirror

Are you ready to learn more about your eyes? Let's look into the mirror again. Do you see the dark circle in the center of your eyes? This is called the pupil. The pupil allows light to travel into your eyes so that you can see. When it is bright around you, the pupil becomes smaller. This protects your eyes from bright light. When it is dark, the pupil becomes bigger so that more light can pass through. This allows you to see when there isn't very much light. What an amazing design God gave our eyes!

When we learned about our sense of hearing, we also learned that God's creation was broken by sin. Things are no longer perfect in our world, and sometimes our bodies aren't able to work quite the way God designed them to. When this happens, a person may have a hard time seeing, or they may not be able to see at all.

But God gave people wisdom and creativity so that we can help others. Some people use the talents and interests God gave them to become eye doctors. We call eye doctors optometrists. An optometrist can help someone find the right pair of glasses. Glasses help people who cannot see very well to be able to see much better. Do you know anyone who wears glasses?

Teacher tip: Allow student to answer.

Other times, a person's eyes may not be able to see anything at all. When a person is not able to see, they are blind. Someone who is blind can use tools like a cane or a guide dog to help them. A cane is a long pole that a person can use to help them feel what is around them as they walk. Guide dogs work hard to focus so they can "see" for blind people.

Someone who is blind may also use a specially trained dog called a guide dog. People use their talents and abilities to train guide dogs to help people. A guide dog wears a special harness with a handle. A person can hold onto the handle, and the guide dog leads the person safely through their home, or even a busy city. A guide dog uses their eyes to keep someone who cannot see safe. Dogs can be helpful creatures!

People can use their talents and abilities to help others. What is one way you can help others? Draw a picture of you helping someone below.

Taking Care of Me 1

Day 1

The Adventures of Gideon and Mr. Snuggly

Hi again! Are you ready for another science adventure? I'm waiting for Mom to get Mr. Snuggly out of the dryer. You see, I accidentally dropped Mr. Snuggly in a big mud puddle earlier. He was covered in stinky, slimy mud and really needed to be washed. I helped Mom gather up my laundry so that we could wash my clothes and Mr. Snuggly in the washing machine. Once the washing machine was done, she put Mr. Snuggly in the dryer to make him soft and dry again.

I take care of Mr. Snuggly and help to keep him clean. Mr. Snuggly is my favorite teddy bear after all! Hmm, I wonder if there are ways I can take care of myself too? Let's explore taking care of ourselves today!

When we began our first science adventure together, we learned that God made you. God created your body.

Teacher tip: You may review Psalm 139:13–14 with your student if desired.

You use your body as you learn, play, and help others. It is important to take good care of your body. When you take good care of your body,

- ☑ Fine glitter
- ☐ Plate
- ☐ Hand towel
- ☐ Sink
- ☐ Hand soap

▶ **Weekly materials list**

you help to keep it clean, safe, and healthy. Can you think of any ways you may be able to take care of yourself?

Teacher tip: Allow student to answer.

One important way that we take care of ourselves is by washing our hands. We touch many things with our hands, and some things may have dirt and germs on them. Germs can make us sick. But when we wash our hands, we can wash away germs! Let's have some fun to see how this works.

Activity directions:

1. Sprinkle glitter onto the plate. Then, help your student press the fronts and backs of their hands into the glitter. Glitter should stick to your student's hands. Compare the glitter to dirt or germs on our hands that we cannot always see.

Let's put your hands under the faucet quickly and see how much glitter washes away.

2. Turn on the faucet and set it to warm water. Help your student place their hands under the stream for 5 seconds. The student should not rub their hands together.
3. Examine their hands together.

How much glitter is left on your hands? Do you think your hands are clean? Would you like to eat a meal with your hands?

We're going to wash our hands again, but this time we will use soap and rub our hands together while we count to 20.

Teacher tip: If your student knows how to count to 10, you can count to 10 twice or sing the alphabet song together instead.

4. Squirt hand soap onto your student's hands and help them rub their hands together under the water for 20 seconds.
5. Dry their hands.

Do you think your hands are clean? Would you like to eat a meal with your hands? Were your hands cleaned better with just water, or by water, soap, and scrubbing?

name _____

In our last adventure together, we saw that water, soap, and scrubbing our hands is the best way to wash dirt and germs away. It is important to wash our hands before we eat, after using the bathroom, and after we get home from being somewhere. Keeping our hands clean helps to keep us healthy!

Another way to take good care of ourselves is by keeping our hands away from our eyes and out of our mouth and nose. This keeps any germs on our hands from being able to get inside of our body.

Now, let me see your smile! Our teeth help us to speak and chew our food; they are very helpful. Teeth can get dirty too, so it is important to brush them in the morning and before bed. Brushing your teeth with a toothbrush and toothpaste helps to keep them clean and healthy.

Our hair and body can also get dirty as we run around and play. We take a bath or shower to clean our hair and body. We wash our hair and body with soap to help the dirt wash away. After a bath or shower, we can get dressed in clean clothes or pajamas. Once you're dressed, don't forget to brush your hair with a comb or hairbrush. These are all ways we can take good care of ourselves!

Washing our hands is one important way we can take good care of ourselves. Color the picture below.

Taking Care of Me 2

week 8

Day

The Adventures of Gideon and Mr. Snuggly

Welcome, friend! Did you enjoy learning some of the ways we can take care of our bodies? I know I did! I've been using my imagination to play with Mr. Snuggly today. Right before you came, I was pretending to cook some yummy cheese quesadillas for us to eat. I love to eat cheese quesadillas with a little salsa and sour cream!

Did you know that eating healthy food is another way we can take good care of our body? Mom and I are going to talk about food today, would you like to join us? Let's get started!

Our bodies need energy to help us grow strong and healthy. We also need energy to run, play, and learn. When we eat food, it gives our body the energy it needs. Food is important to our bodies!

In order to keep our bodies strong and healthy, we need to make sure that we eat good, healthy food. Good food, like fruits and vegetables, gives our body the energy it needs. Other healthy foods like milk, eggs, cheese, bread, and meat also give our body good energy.

Foods like cookies, chips, and candy all taste very good, but they don't give our bodies the best kind of energy. We can enjoy these foods sometimes, but we want to make sure we give our bodies good food each day. God created many different kinds of foods, each with unique flavors we can taste. Sometimes, we eat a food all by itself — like an apple! Other times, we use our creativity to combine several foods together and create something new. For example, we can chop onions, tomatoes, and peppers together to create a salsa. Or, we can fry rice, eggs, chicken, and vegetables together to make delicious fried rice.

Can you think of something you've eaten all by itself?

Teacher tip: Allow student to answer. If they are unsure, talk about a fruit or vegetable you've eaten by itself.

We can enjoy many types of food. We can also try new foods and taste new flavors. We may not always like everything we try, but it is fun to taste something different!

God created fruits and vegetables with beautiful colors and yummy flavors! Color the apple, strawberry, cherry, and tomato red; the pear green; and you can use orange to color the orange and carrot.

name _____

We've been learning about ways we can take good care of the bodies God gave us. Can you remember some of the ways we can take good care of ourselves?

Teacher tip: Allow student to answer. Answers may include washing hands, brushing teeth, bathing, eating good food.

Let's talk about another way we can take good care of ourselves and others today! Have you ever scraped your knee, cut your finger, or bumped your leg hard?

Teacher tip: Allow student to answer.

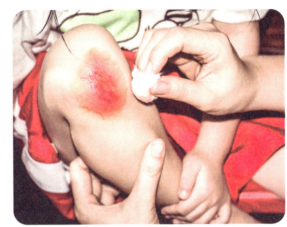

When our bodies are hurt, they may bleed, bruise, or begin to swell. When accidents happen and someone is hurt, we can be ready to help. When someone's skin is scraped or cut, it can be painful and may even bleed. A cut or scrape can also be called a wound. When a wound bleeds, the blood helps to clean and protect it.

We can also help our bodies heal and protect a wound by gently rinsing it with running water from the sink. We can also use mild soap to help clean the wound. Once it is clean, we can dry the wound with a clean cotton pad and then put a band-aid on to protect it.

materials needed
- [ ] Band-aid
- [ ] Sink
- [ ] Clean towel or cotton pad
- [ ] Optional: mild soap
- [ ] Optional: washable red marker

When we fall or bump our skin on something, it can cause a bruise or swelling. We can use an ice pack to help the pain go away. It's important to wrap an ice pack in a towel before putting it on our skin — the ice is too cold all by itself!

Adventures in the World Around Me ▸ Week 8

Accidents happen — but we can make sure we're ready to help when someone gets hurt. Let's practice being helpful together.

Activity directions:

Optional: If desired, you can use a washable red marker to draw a small "cut" on your hand.

Let's pretend I have a small cut on my hand. First, we need to make sure the wound is clean. Can you help me gently rinse the wound?

1. Guide your student to the sink.

Can you help me rinse the cut? You can also apply mild soap if you want.

Now that the wound is clean, it's time to dry it. We'll need to use a clean cotton pad to gently pat it dry. Can you gently dry the pretend cut?

2. Once dried, help your student apply a band-aid to the wound.

Thank you for your help!

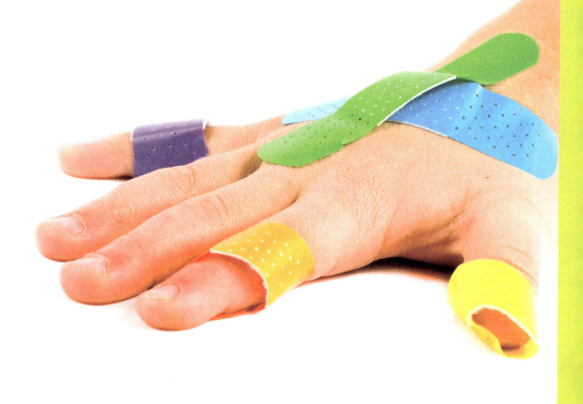

Tools We Use in Science

week 9

Day 1

The Adventures of Gideon and Mr. Snuggly

I'm glad you're here, friend! I have my magnifying glass in my hand, and I'm going to use it to look closely at a leaf. A magnifying glass makes things look bigger, which helps us to see small things better. A magnifying glass is one tool we can use to help us study science. I feel like a real scientist when I use my magnifying glass to explore creation!

Did you know that there are many tools scientists use to study the world around them? Let's learn more about the tools we use to explore the world God made!

Science helps us to explore the world that God made and learn more about Him. There are many tools we can use to explore, observe, examine, and measure things around us as we study science.

Did you know that our five senses are tools we can use as we explore science? They are! We use our eyes to carefully observe and examine what we can see. We use our ears to listen to things around us. Our hands and our sense of touch help us explore and feel things. We can use our nose to smell things as we learn — and sometimes, we can even taste things we are learning about!

Apple	✓
Cutting board	☐
Knife (adult only)	☐

▶ **Weekly materials list**

Our five senses are very helpful science tools. Let's use our five senses today to help us learn more about an apple.

Activity directions:

1. Give your student the apple.

   - What does it feel like? Is it smooth or rough? Big or small? Hard or soft?
   - What color is the apple?
   - What does it smell like?
   - How many seeds do you think are inside the apple?

Let's continue examining this apple. I'm going to cut it into slices, and we'll count the seeds. Listen carefully as I cut the apple — what do you hear? Can you describe the sound to me?

2. Carefully slice the apple and remove the seeds. Count them with your student.

Are there more or less seeds than you thought there would be?

3. Give the slices to your student.

   - What does the inside of the apple feel like?
   - What does it smell like?
   - What color is the inside of the apple? Is it a different color than the outside?
   - What does the apple taste like? Is it sweet or sour?
   - Does it feel hard or soft when you take a bite?
   - What did you learn about the apple?

name

Wasn't it fun to explore the apple as we used our five senses to learn more about it? We can study science through our five senses, but there are many other helpful tools we can use as well. Let's talk about other science tools today.

materials needed
- [ ] Magnifying glass
- [ ] Ruler

We can look through a magnifying glass to help us see small things better. A magnifying glass makes things appear bigger to our eyes. We can use a magnifying glass to look closely at a leaf, flower, or insect. A magnifying glass can help us see things that our eyes have a hard time seeing all by themselves.

Sometimes we need to measure things as we explore science. There are several tools that can measure different things. A ruler can measure how long or short something is. A thermometer measures the temperature, or how cold or hot it is. A scale can help us measure how much something weighs.

Other helpful science tools are crayons, pencils, markers, and paper. As scientists study the world, they write down or draw the things they've learned about. This helps them to share what they've learned with others! As you explore the world around you, you can draw the things you see and share them with others too.

Oh, no! The letters on our worksheet are too small. Use your magnifying glass to help you see the letters. Can you tell me what letters you see?

A B C D E

Measure each creature below with the ruler. Then circle the one that is the longest.

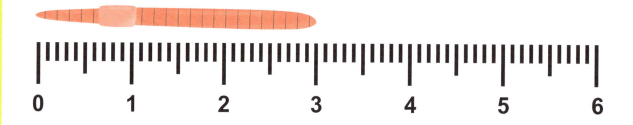

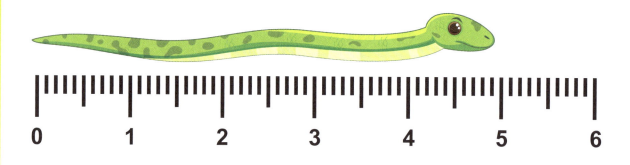

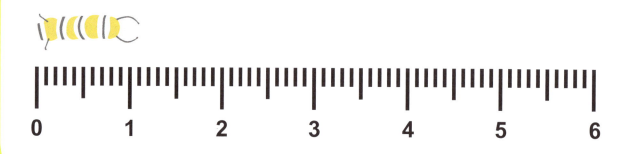

Light and Shadows

week 10

Day

The Adventures of Gideon and Mr. Snuggly

Hi there! I'm excited you're here. Do you remember what we've learned about in our last few lessons? We've explored our five senses, how to take good care of ourselves, and about some of the tools we can use to study science. Now, it's time for another science adventure together!

I'm going to learn about light and shadows today. Would you like to join me? I have my flashlight right here and ready to go. Mom said we're going to use it to make shadows of Mr. Snuggly! That sounds like fun. Hmm, I wonder when light was created? Let's see if we can find the answer!

When we read the Bible, we learn that God created the heavens and the earth in six days — and on the seventh day, God rested. Do you know which of those days light was created on? We can find the answer in the Bible. Listen carefully as I read, and see if you hear the answer to our question: What day was light created on?

Teacher tip: Emphasize the last sentence in the passage.

| Flashlight | ✓ |
| Opaque object such as a book or stuffed animal | ☐ |

▶ Weekly materials list

In the beginning, God created the heavens and the earth. The earth didn't have any shape. And it was empty. There was darkness over the surface of the waves. At that time, the Spirit of God was hovering over the waters. God said, 'Let there be light.' And there was light. God saw that the light was good. He separated the light from the darkness. God called the light 'day.' He called the darkness 'night.' There was evening, and there was morning. It was day one (Genesis 1:1–5).

Did you hear the answer to our question? God created light on the first day of creation. Light is an important part of creation. It allows us to see things during the day. Light also provides heat to warm the earth and the energy plants need to grow. Can you think of something that gives us light?

Teacher tip: Allow student to answer.

On the fourth day of creation, God created the sun. God designed the sun to give us the perfect amount of light and heat on the earth. Can you imagine what the earth would be like without the sun?

Teacher tip: Allow student to answer. You may also imagine with them.

The sun is an important source of light. Many other things also give us light. Circle the objects that have light.

name

Did you know that light doesn't sit still in one place? If we turn on a flashlight, the light travels out from the flashlight. Light travels out from its source unless it reaches something that blocks its path.

materials needed
- Flashlight
- Opaque object such as a book or stuffed animal

Have you ever stepped outside on a sunny day and noticed shadows on the ground from the buildings, leaves, or tree branches above? When something blocks the path of light, a dark shadow is created. Some objects can block light from traveling any farther, but some objects cannot.

Objects that are clear, like glass windows, cannot stop light from traveling through them. When an object cannot block or stop light, we say it is transparent. We can see through things that are transparent. Look out a window; what do you see on the other side?

Teacher tip: Allow student to answer.

When an object is not transparent, we cannot see through it. Objects like a book, stuffed animal, or tree branch are not transparent. These objects block light from traveling any farther. When light cannot travel through something, we say the object is opaque. Things that are opaque create shadows. Let's use some opaque objects to create shadows today!

Activity directions:

1. Go into a darkened room with your student.
2. Have your student turn the flashlight on and shine it onto the floor or wall.

Can you see the light? Is anything blocking the light's path?

3. Now, hold an opaque object several inches to a foot in front of the flashlight.

Now what do you see?

4. The student should mention the shadow.

The light could not pass through our opaque object. Since it blocked the light, a shadow was created!

5. Use other solid objects to create unique shadows.

Optional: Use your hands to create shadow puppets with your student, such as the ones below.

Primary and Secondary Colors

week 11

Day

The Adventures of Gideon and Mr. Snuggly

Why hello, friend! I've been waiting for you to come. I want to tell you all about the things I've seen today.

This morning, I saw bright red strawberries in my cereal. They tasted really yummy!

After breakfast, it was time to help my mom take a letter out to the mailbox. I put on my orange shoes and blue coat. Then I grabbed Mr. Snuggly, and we walked out the door together. The sun was shining bright, and I noticed the clear, blue sky above our heads. When I looked down, I saw that Mom's pretty yellow daffodils were blooming in her garden!

There are many different colors all around us. That gives me an idea! Let's learn more about the colors we can see today. Are you ready to get started?

From the clear, blue sky to the bright, green grass, there are colors all around us. God gave us many colors to enjoy. We can eat a red raspberry, look out at the blue ocean, smell a beautiful purple flower, eat a juicy orange, watch a yellow finch fly, and feel the green grass under our feet. What is your favorite color?

Weekly materials list

- [✓] 6 cotton swabs
- [ ] Washable red, blue, and yellow paint
- [ ] Paper
- [ ] Plastic tablecloth

Teacher tip: Allow student to answer. You may also share your favorite color.

Some colors are made by mixing two colors together. Other colors cannot be made by mixing colors together. Red, yellow, and blue are colors that cannot be made by mixing any other colors together. We call red, yellow, and blue primary colors. Primary colors are important because we can mix them together to create other colors — we'll be talking more about that soon. In the meantime, let's go on a color scavenger hunt!

Can you find one thing in your house that is red, one that is yellow, and one that is blue? Once you find something red, yellow, and blue, draw an X in the small box. Then draw a picture of what you found.

☐ I found something **red!**

☐ I found something **yellow!**

☐ I found something **blue!**

name

We're learning about colors this week. I'm excited to explore more colors today! Last time, we learned that red, yellow, and blue are called primary colors. Primary colors cannot be made by mixing two colors together. But primary colors do make other colors when we mix them together.

materials needed
- ☐ 6 cotton swabs
- ☐ Washable red, blue, and yellow paint
- ☐ Paper
- ☐ Plastic tablecloth

For example, we can mix blue and yellow together to create green. When red and blue are mixed together, it creates the color purple. Hmm, what if we mix red and yellow together — are you able to guess what color red and yellow would make?

Teacher tip: Allow student to answer.

When we mix them together, red and yellow create the color orange! Green, purple, and orange are called secondary colors. Secondary colors are made when we mix two primary colors together.

Let's have some fun mixing primary colors together to create secondary colors!

Activity directions:

1. Cover the table with the tablecloth to protect it.
2. Open the paint containers, or squirt some of each color of paint onto a plate.
3. Give your student two cotton swabs. Have them dip the first swab in the blue paint, then use it to paint a circle on the paper.
4. Have them dip the second swab into the yellow paint, then paint over the blue circle they've created.

Describe to me what happened.

5. Next, give the student two new cotton swabs and repeat this process with the blue and red paint.

What color was created?

6. Finally, give the student two new cotton swabs and repeat with red and yellow.

What color was created?

7. Give the student a clean sheet of paper and have them paint a picture.

Describe your picture to me. What colors do you see?

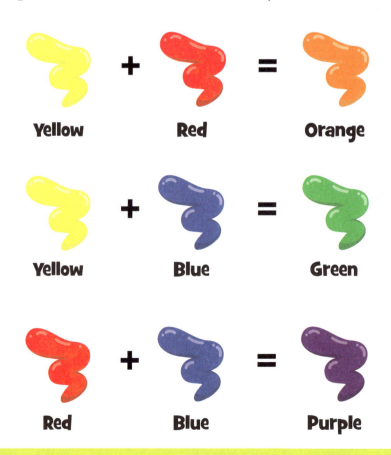

Yellow	Red	Orange
Yellow	Blue	Green
Red	Blue	Purple

Size

week 12

Day

The Adventures of Gideon and Mr. Snuggly

Hello, friend! I enjoyed learning about primary and secondary colors on our last adventure. Did you have fun? Today, I would like to create an imaginary story about Mr. Snuggly. Let's see. . . "One bright summer day, Mr. Snuggly decided to climb an apple tree and pick the biggest apple. But there was one problem. The biggest apple was. . . ."

Hmm, I need to describe where the apple was on the tree. Can you think of a way to describe where the apple was? Ooh, I have an idea. "The biggest apple was high up on the tall tree." I'm going to need to describe more things in my story. Let's talk about the words we can use to describe size today!

We can use words to describe the colors we see, the size of something, and even its shape! We talked about colors on our last adventure, and we'll talk more about different shapes soon. For today, let's learn about the words we can use to talk about the size of something.

Tall, short, big, small, light, heavy, large, thin, wide, huge, and tiny are some of the words we can use to describe something's size. Let's think about a tree — what words would you use to describe the size of a tree?

An assortment of objects that are of small, medium, and large sizes

Weekly materials list

Adventures in the World Around Me ▶ Week 12

Teacher tip: Allow student to answer.

As we explore the world God created through science, we can use words like these to share what we see or learn about with others. For example, do you remember the apple we cut up during one of our adventures?

Teacher tip: Allow student to answer.

- How would you describe the apple? Do you think it was small or large?
- Did the apple feel heavy or light in your hands?

Let's practice looking at items and describing their size. I have some small, medium, and large things here. We can describe them and sort them into groups by their size.

Activity directions:

1. Lay out the objects for the student to examine.
2. Have the student pick something that is small and help them describe the object.

- How does it feel?
- What color is it?
- How would you describe it?

3. Have the student place it in the small pile.
4. Repeat for each different object and sort by size: small, medium, or large.

name _____

Welcome back! We're learning about words we can use to describe something's size. Tall, short, big, small, light, heavy, large, thin, wide, huge, and tiny are all words we can use.

Do you remember the story Gideon started to imagine about Mr. Snuggly? Let's read it again. "One bright summer day, Mr. Snuggly decided to climb an apple tree and pick the biggest apple. But there was one problem. The biggest apple was high up on the tall tree."

How would you finish Mr. Snuggly's adventure story? Can you think of any more words we could use to describe sizes in the story?

Teacher tip: Allow student to answer. You may also guide them in a way to finish the story.

Here is how Gideon imagined his story:

"One bright summer day, Mr. Snuggly decided to climb an apple tree and pick the **biggest** apple. But there was one problem. The **biggest** apple was high up on the **tall** tree. Mr. Snuggly slowly climbed the apple tree. He was very careful once he reached the **thin** branches near the top! Finally, Mr. Snuggly reached the **biggest** apple. He picked the apple and realized it felt **heavy** to him because he is so **small**! Mr. Snuggly carefully climbed back down the tree. Once he reached the bottom, he took a **small** bite of that **big**, juicy apple. Yum!"

Let's look at a few pictures of different objects together and decide what word would describe them the best. Once we decide on the word, you can circle it!

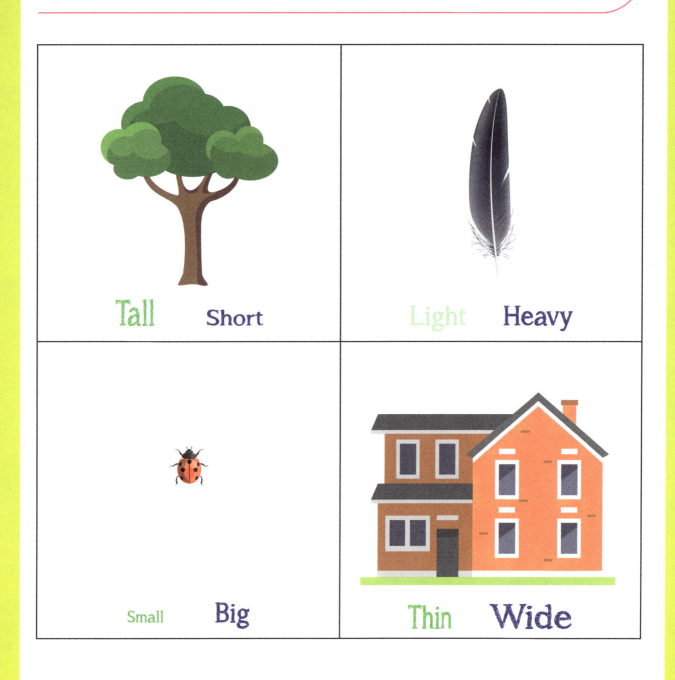

Shape

Day

The Adventures of Gideon and Mr. Snuggly

Hi! Just a minute, friend, I need to take off my rubber boots. We got home from visiting my friend Chloe a few minutes ago. Chloe lives on a farm. Her family has a big red barn and many different farm animals like chickens, ducks, pigs, horses, and cows! Chloe's dog Pickles likes to play with Mr. Snuggly — but he gets my stuffed animal all slobbery. Yuck!

While we were at the farm today, I noticed many different shapes all around me. The barn doors looked like big rectangles. There was a cat inside the barn, and her ears were shaped like triangles! Then we saw some baby piglets. Their little noses looked like ovals. There are shapes all around — let's explore them together today!

 In our last adventure, we learned about the words we use to describe the size of something. We also have special words we use to describe how something is shaped. For example, when we see a round shape, we call it a **circle**. Dinner plates, car tires, and coins are all in the shape of a circle. Can you think of anything else in our home that is a circle?

Teacher tip: Allow student to answer.

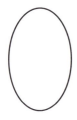  **Ovals** are similar to circles, but they look like they were smooshed. Balloons often have an oval shape, and you may notice some types of leaves also have an oval shape.

  When four straight lines connect together, they form a **square**. In a square, each of the lines is the same size. You might find a square-shaped box or picture frame. Sometimes, even windows have square shapes!

  **Rectangles** are similar to squares, but they have two short lines and two longer lines. Rectangles look very similar to squares, but they are longer on one side. Your ruler is a rectangle. If you look at the door of your house, you may also find one big rectangle!

  When three lines connect and form points, we call the shape a **triangle**. Sometimes a triangle's lines are all the same size. Other times, the lines are different sizes, but it is still a triangle! Let's practice recognizing shapes!

Color the circles red, the squares blue, the rectangles orange, the triangles green, and the ovals purple.

Day

God placed many shapes throughout creation. As you explore the world around you, you may notice circles, triangles, squares, rectangles, and ovals on plants, animals, fish, and buildings. Let's look closely at this flower. Can you see any shapes in it?

I see a yellow circle in the center, and the white petals on the outside are shaped like triangles! It is fun to look for shapes around us — let's see how many different shapes we can find around our house.

Activity directions:

1. Begin by looking for something in the shape of a circle. The kitchen cupboards are a great place to start. Hint: check plates, cups, bowls, and cabinet hardware.

How many circles can you find?

2. Look for an oval shape next. Hint: check baking dishes and spoons for oval shapes.

How many ovals can you find?

3. Now, look around your home for square shapes. Windows, decorative doors, cube storage, blocks, and children's books are good places to look.

How many squares can you find?

4. Next, look for rectangle shapes. Hint: check doors, baking trays, calendars, and books.

How many rectangles can you find?

5. Finally, look around your home for triangles. If you have a pet, check their ears for a triangle shape. Building toys, pie servers, and plant leaves can be great places to look.

How many triangles can you find?

Can you find a circle, triangle, square, rectangle, and oval in the picture? Circle the shapes you see.

Exploring My World

week 14

Day

The Adventures of Gideon and Mr. Snuggly

Welcome back, friend! I've been playing outside with Mr. Snuggly today. I found a pretty flower in Mom's garden while we were out there! Mom gave me permission to pick it. She said that I could look at it closely like a real scientist.

I'm going to use my magnifying glass to examine this flower. Then I'm going to use what we've learned about color, size, and shape to describe the flower to Dad when he gets home tonight! Would you like to come along? Let's get started!

God created many things that we can explore, examine, and learn about in the world around us. Examine is a big word that means to look closely at something. A scientist's job is to explore, examine, and learn about the world God created. Scientists have many tools they can use to do their job — and you have tools you can use as well! Do you remember some of the science tools you can use?

Teacher tip: Allow student to answer. You may remind them of the five senses, magnifying glass, and ruler.

Weekly materials list
- A flower ☐
- Ruler ☐
- Magnifying glass ☐

We can use our science tools to help us learn more about God's creation, just like a real scientist. Let's examine a flower together and see what we can discover and learn about it.

Activity directions:

1. Place the flower on the table and give your student the worksheet.

Look carefully at the flower. What colors do you see?

2. Help them complete section #1 on the worksheet. Your student may use crayons to scribble the colors they see.

Look carefully at the shape of the flower. Are there any shapes you recognize, such as a circle, square, rectangle, oval, or triangle?

3. Help them circle any shapes they see in section #2 of the worksheet.

Look carefully at the stem on the flower. Is the stem long or short?

4. Help them circle their answer on section #3 of the worksheet. Next, help your student measure the full length of the flower with the ruler. If needed, help them write the answer for section #4.

Look carefully at the flower's petals. What are they shaped like? Are there a lot of petals or only a few?

5. Help your student answer sections #5 and #6 on the worksheet.
6. Give your student the magnifying glass and help them look closely at the flower.

Do you notice anything else interesting?

Smell the flower. What does it smell like?

1. I see these colors on the flower:

2. I see these shapes in the flower:

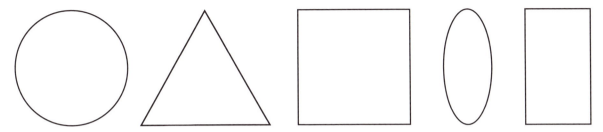

3. The flower's stem is:

   Long   **Short**

4. The flower is _____ inches tall.

5. The flower's petals look like this:

6. The flower has **a lot / a few** petals.

Day

It was a lot of fun to examine the flower and write down the things we noticed! When we write down, or record, the things we notice, it helps us to remember what we saw. It also helps us to tell other people about something we noticed or discovered in God's creation. Scientists take pictures, write things down, and share the things they learn about God's creation.

As we explore the world around us through science, we discover and learn about new things. Learning about new things is fun and exciting. The things we learn about can change, but what God has told us in the Bible is always the same. Isaiah 40:8 tells us,

The grass dries up. The flowers fall to the ground. But what our God says will stand forever.

As we learn and discover through science, we know that God's Word is truth that will never change. Speaking of flowers, do you remember the flower we examined the other day? Can you draw a picture of it? You can look back at the notes we made about the flower in our last lesson to remind you of what we saw. After you've drawn the flower, be sure to show it to someone else and tell them all about what you learned.

Draw the flower you examined below.

Water

> week 15

Day

The Adventures of Gideon and Mr. Snuggly

Why, hello there! We just got back from the swimming pool in our community. I couldn't take Mr. Snuggly into the water with me, but I sure had fun swimming and splashing! On the way home, Mom and I talked about all the ways we use water. I need water to drink, Mom uses water to cook, we use water to wash our hands, to clean, and sometimes even to play with during the hot summer.

We need water for lots of different things. I'd like to learn more about water today. Would you like to join me? Here we go!

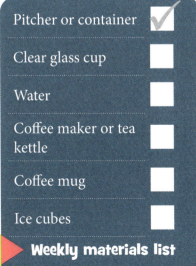

Water is important. People, plants, animals, and fish all need water in order to live. God designed the earth to hold the water we need. Can you think of any places you might see water outside?

Teacher tip: Allow student to answer.

We see water on the earth in streams, rivers, ponds, lakes, and the ocean. Today, I think it would be fun to use our five senses to learn more about water together. Let's talk about what we think water is like first, then we will use our five senses to see if we are right!

- [✓] Pitcher or container
- [ ] Clear glass cup
- [ ] Water
- [ ] Coffee maker or tea kettle
- [ ] Coffee mug
- [ ] Ice cubes

▶ Weekly materials list

Teacher tip: Give your student this worksheet. Help your student answer the questions in the What I Think section. They can circle the answer they select.

Science helps us to test the things that we think about something to see if we are right or not. Now it's time to explore water to see if what we think about it is true.

Activity directions:

Listen carefully as I pour water into the glass cup from the pitcher. Describe what pouring water sounds like.

Smell the water in the glass.

Another word for smell is odor. Does the water have an odor? Clean water does not have a smell or odor. Clean water is odorless.

What color is the water?

Clean water is clear; it does not have a color. Another way to say that is the water is colorless.

Taste the water. Does it have any taste?

Clean water usually does not have a strong taste. It may not taste like anything to you.

Dip your fingers into the glass to feel the water. Describe what water feels like.

Wasn't it fun to explore water together? Now it's time to record what we found, just like a real scientist.

What I Think:

Does water have a taste? Yes / No

Does water have a color? Yes / No

Does water have a smell? Yes / No

What I Found:

Does water have a taste? Yes / No

Does water have a color? Yes / No

Does water have a smell? Yes / No

Day name

Now that we've explored water together, it's time to learn a little more about it! Water is a liquid. A liquid can be poured and splashed, like milk or juice. A liquid can also fill up something else, like a glass or a pitcher.

materials needed
- [ ] Water
- [ ] Coffee maker or tea kettle
- [ ] Coffee mug
- [ ] Ice cubes

We often see water when it is a liquid — but did you know water can be in other states as well? State is a word that means the way something exists, or how we see it. Water can also be a solid. Solids are things like wood or dinner plates; they can't be poured or splashed. Frozen, cold ice is water in a solid state.

Water can also be a gas. Gases float through the air. When steam rises from a hot cup of coffee, tea, or hot chocolate, this is water in a gas state. Water can be a liquid, solid, or gas. Let's explore these states of water together.

Activity directions:

1. Teacher, use the coffee maker or tea kettle to warm the water to steaming hot.
2. Pour the hot water into the coffee mug until it is about half-full. Observe the steam with your student.

The steam is water in a gas state. The water inside the mug is in a liquid state.

Teacher tip: Make sure to warn your student that hot water is dangerous. They should only observe the water and not touch the cup or water.

3. Give your student an ice cube.

The ice cube is made of water in a solid state — it is frozen.

What will happen to the ice cube if we place it into the cup of hot water?

4. Pick up an ice cube and carefully place it into the coffee mug. Observe what happens.

The ice cube melted, and the water returned to a liquid state.

Solid

Gas

Liquid

Heat

week 16

Day

The Adventures of Gideon and Mr. Snuggly

Hello! I'm glad you're back for another science adventure. I woke up really early today — the sun wasn't even up yet!

When I went to the kitchen with Mr. Snuggly, I found that my dad was already up and getting ready for work. I gave him a big good morning hug and watched him as he made his coffee.

Dad poured cold water from the sink into the tea kettle. Then he turned on the kitchen stove and the fire began to make the water in the kettle warm. Once the water was hot, Dad carefully poured the water into his mug to make the coffee. He made me a mug of hot chocolate too!

I noticed that the fire made heat and the heat changed the water from cold to hot. I thought that was interesting! Let's learn more about heat and how it changes things today.

God created the sun, moon, and stars on the fourth day of creation. Can you think of any ways the sun helps the earth?

- Your favorite cookie recipe
- Ingredients and supplies for recipe

▶ **Weekly materials list**

Teacher tip: Allow student to answer.

God designed the sun to give us the perfect amount of light and heat on the earth. Without heat from the sun, it would be far too cold to live on the earth! The sun is a big source of light and heat, but there are also smaller sources that we receive light and heat from. Can you think of anything else that gives us light and heat?

Teacher tip: Allow student to answer.

We receive light and heat from things like candles, lightbulbs, fire, and electricity. A kitchen stove uses fire or electricity to heat and cook our food. A campfire can give us light on a dark night and keep us warm when the air is chilly.

Did you know that heat can also change things? Heat can change cold water into hot water, hard spaghetti into soft spaghetti, and gooey batter into a yummy cake. That gives me an idea — let's use heat today to change dough into cookies!

Activity directions:

1. Prepare your space and the ingredients you'll need to make the cookies with your student.
2. Make the recipe with your student. Have them help measure, pour, mix, and shape the cookies if applicable. As you prepare the recipe, have your student describe what they see, hear, smell, and see throughout the process.
3. Once the cookies are on the baking tray, have your student describe the dough.

How do you think the heat in the oven will change the cookies?

4. Once your cookies have finished baking and have cooled, have your student examine them. Enjoy a cookie with your student.

How did heat change the cookies?

name _____

It was fun to see how heat changed our cookie dough, but I think I enjoyed eating the cookies the most! Heat is an important part of creation. We need heat to keep ourselves warm when the weather is cold, to cook food, and to warm water for a shower. Can you think of anything else we use heat for?

Teacher tip: Allow student to answer. If your student cannot think of anything, you can mention how a clothes or hairdryer uses heat to do a job.

Heat often changes things around us. The heat from the sun can change fluffy, white snow into puddles of water. Hot water can melt ice cubes. The heat from the oven can bake cookies or roast our dinner. The heat in a clothes dryer can dry our clothes. The heat from a furnace keeps our home warm. The heat from a campfire can toast a marshmallow. Can you think of any other ways we use heat to change things?

Teacher tip: Allow student to answer. If your student cannot think of anything, you can mention how a toaster uses heat to make toast.

Heat is an important part of creation, and it's fun to think about all the ways it changes things! But don't forget to be very careful around things that can make heat. Very hot things can burn our skin if we get too close. It's important to always be careful around hot things.

We can receive heat from many different things. Circle the things that can give us heat.

Living and Non-Living

week 17

Day

The Adventures of Gideon and Mr. Snuggly

I'm glad you came today, friend. I have a lot to talk about with you! We went to the lake yesterday. I splashed in the water and created my very own sandcastle. I imagined Mr. Snuggly was the king of the sandcastle. It was fun!

After I built the castle, I walked around the lake with my mom and sister. We saw a few wildflowers, a swimming fish, a tiny turtle, and smooth stones. I noticed that some things, like the turtle, are alive, but other things, like the smooth stones, are not. Mom said we could talk about living and non-living things today. Would you like to join us? Let's get started!

God created many living things. People, animals, birds, insects, fish, and plants are all living things. God also created many things that are not alive. When something is not alive, we can also say it is non-living. Things like dirt, rocks, water, and toys are not alive. But how can we tell what things are alive and what things are not alive? Let's talk more about that!

Living things can move by themselves. You move as you run, jump, and play. You are a living thing. Animals, birds, insects, and fish also move around by

Stuffed animal, baby doll, or action figure

▶ **Weekly materials list**

Adventures in the World Around Me ....▶ Week 17

77

themselves. Plants do not have a body like people, birds, or fish, but the flower petals and leaves can move slightly so that the plant can receive more sunlight. Although plants are alive, the Bible tells us that plants do not have the breath of life like people and animals do.

Living things need food. Food gives us nutrients that we need to live and grow. People, animals, birds, insects, and fish all need to eat food to stay healthy and strong. Plants do not have a mouth, but they do absorb nutrients from the ground through their roots.

Living things can grow. Did you know that I was once the same size as you? It's true! I was once a baby, but I've grown up. You are growing too. Puppies grow into dogs, kittens grow into cats, small fish grow into larger fish, a baby grasshopper grows bigger, and baby birds grow into adult birds. A tiny seed grows to become a big plant.

These are a few of the ways we can tell if something is living. We'll talk more about another way in our next lesson. For today, let's practice finding living things.

Circle the pictures of living things. If you're not sure, you can ask: Does it move by itself? Does it need food? Does it grow?

name _____

In our last lesson, we learned that living things can move by themselves, they need food, and they can grow. Can you think of anything else living things can do?

Teacher tip: Allow student to answer.

materials needed
☐ Stuffed animal, baby doll, or action figure

Living things need air to breathe. God designed people, animals, insects, birds, and plants to breathe in different ways. You and I breathe air through our nose. Take a deep breath in. Can you feel the air move through your nose?

Teacher tip: Allow student to answer.

Animals and birds also breathe through their nose or beak. God designed insects with tiny holes in their body called spiracles. Insects use the spiracles to breathe. God also gave fish a unique way to breathe. Fish have gills instead of noses. As water passes through the fish's gills, they absorb the air in the water. What an amazing design!

But what about plants? Plants do not have noses, gills, or spiracles, but they are living things. So, how do plants breathe? Plants absorb air through their leaves in a special process called photosynthesis.

If something can move by itself, needs food to survive, can grow, and needs to breathe air, it is a living thing. People, animals, insects, birds, fish, and plants are all living things. If something cannot move by itself, does not need food to survive, cannot grow, and does not need air to breathe, it is non-living. Books, toys, dishes, rocks, and boxes are examples of non-living things.

Activity directions:

Give your student the stuffed animal, baby doll, or action figure.

Is this item living or non-living? Explain why it is non-living. Remember that this item cannot move by itself, does not need food, cannot grow, and does not need to breathe.

Bonus: What real thing does the toy represent (for example, a person or particular animal). Is the real thing living or non-living? Explain why.

Living things can move, need food, can grow, and need to breathe air. Draw a picture of a living thing.

Non-living things cannot move by themselves, do not need food, do not grow, and do not need to breathe. Draw a picture of a non-living thing.

Plants

week 18

Day 1

The Adventures of Gideon and Mr. Snuggly

Hello there! I'm getting ready to go outside and help Mom in her garden. My mom has many different plants in her garden. There are beautiful flowers, long vines, and vegetable plants! I like to smell the pretty flowers in her garden. Once the vegetables are ripe, we get to pick and eat them! The sugar snap peas are my favorite ones to eat.

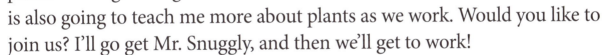

Today, we need to pull the weeds out of her garden. Weeds are plants growing somewhere that they don't belong. When we pull out the weeds, it helps the other plants in the garden grow well. Mom is also going to teach me more about plants as we work. Would you like to join us? I'll go get Mr. Snuggly, and then we'll get to work!

God created many different kinds of plants. Do you know what day of creation God created plants on? Let's read from the Bible to find out! Listen carefully for the answer as I read.

Teacher tip: Emphasize the last sentence in the passage.

Then God said, 'Let the land produce plants. Let them produce their own seeds. And let there be trees on the land that grow fruit with seeds in

Weekly materials list

- Glue stick ✓
- Construction paper ☐
- Packet of seeds (flowers, herbs, etc.) ☐
- Potting soil ☐
- Small pot ☐

it. Let each kind of plant or tree have its own kind of seeds.' And that's exactly what happened. So the land produced plants. Each kind of plant had its own kind of seeds. And the land produced trees that grew fruit with seeds in it. Each kind of tree had its own kind of seeds. God saw that it was good. There was evening, and there was morning. It was day three (Genesis 1:11–13).

Did you hear the answer to our question? God created plants on day three! Some plants are large, and others are quite small. Some plants have beautiful flowers and designs, but others are plain. While plants can look quite different from each other, they all have similar parts. Let's learn the basic parts of a plant together!

We'll start with the first part. We usually cannot see this part because it is under the soil. Plants have roots that grow down into the soil. Roots help to hold the plant in place during wind and rain. That is an important job! Roots also draw water and nutrients into the plant from the soil. Plants need water and nutrients in order to live and grow.

The second part of a plant is the stem. Roots carry water and nutrients to the plant's stem. The stem helps to hold the plant up tall and strong, and it also carries water and nutrients through the plant. Can you think of anything that might be attached to the stem?

Teacher tip: Allow student to answer.

Many plants have leaves attached to the stem. Leaves are the third part of a plant. Leaves absorb air and sunlight and use them to create food for the plant. Plants need air and sunlight in order to grow and live.

Some plants also have flowers. A plant may have one flower at the top of the stem, or it may have many flowers. Flowers can be big or small, brightly colored or plain. Some flowers have a very nice smell; others can be stinky! Flowers are important because they help plants create seeds. We'll talk more about seeds next time!

This plant is all broken apart! Cut out the pieces and then glue the pieces back together in the right order on a piece of construction paper. Remember, the roots grow from the bottom and hold the plant in the soil. The stem grows above the roots, leaves grow from the stem, and the flower grows at the top.

Adventures in the World Around Me ▶ Week 18

Page blank for cutting purposes.

name _____

Day

We learned the basic parts of a plant last time. Wasn't that fun? The roots, stem, leaves, and even flowers all work together so that the plant can grow strong and healthy.

Flowers are an important part of many plants because flowers make seeds. New plants grow from seeds.

materials needed
- [ ] Packet of seeds (flowers, herbs, etc.)
- [ ] Potting soil
- [ ] Small pot

Animals, birds, and the wind help to spread seeds. This helps new plants to grow in different places. Seeds need dirt, water, and sunlight in order to grow. People can gather seeds and use them to plant new flowers, fruits, trees, and vegetables.

We can also plant seeds of our own and watch the new plant grow slowly. Let's plant some seeds today!

Activity directions:

1. Help your student plant the seeds according to the package's directions.
2. Place the pot where it will receive some sunlight.
3. Help your student care for the seeds and watch as they grow.

Trees

> **Day**

The Adventures of Gideon and Mr. Snuggly

Welcome back, friend. I'm excited to learn more about God's creation through science with you! We learned about plants during our last adventure. Did you know that trees are also a type of plant? It's true!

We have a small apple tree in our front yard. I like to climb the tree with Mr. Snuggly. There is a branch that is perfect for Mr. Snuggly to sit on. Sometimes, I climb the tree and watch the birds. Hey, that gives me an idea! I'd like to learn more about trees and birds. Let's explore trees first, and then we can learn about birds later on. Would you like to join me? Let's get started!

Do you remember what day of creation God created plants on?

Teacher tip: Allow student to answer.

God created plants and trees on day three! Trees are much taller than most other types of plants, but they are still a type of plant. Trees have many parts that all work together. Let's talk about the parts of a tree!

Just like plants, trees also have roots. A tree's roots grow deep into the soil and spread wide around the tree. The roots help to hold the tree up tall and strong. The roots also absorb water from the soil, just like other plants' roots.

The second part of a tree is the trunk. A tree's trunk is like a plant's stem, but much bigger and thicker. The trunk helps the tree to grow tall and strong. It also helps to carry water from the roots through the tree. Tree trunks are covered in bark. The bark protects the inside of the tree. Some trees have smooth bark, and other trees have very rough bark.

The third part of the tree is the branches! Branches grow from the tree's trunk. Some branches are thick and strong, and others are quite thin. Leaves or needles grow from the branches. Do you know what job the leaves and needles do for the tree?

Teacher tip: Allow student to answer.

Leaves need to absorb air and sunlight for the tree. The tree can use air and sunlight to make food for itself through a special process God created called photosynthesis.

Many types of trees can grow together in a forest. Color the forest below.

name _____

As scientists learn about God's creation, they organize things into groups. Though God created many different types of trees, scientists organize them into two groups. The first group of trees are called deciduous trees. Deciduous trees have leaves that can be different sizes and shapes. The leaves turn brown, red, yellow, or orange and fall off the tree, usually during the fall season. In the spring, the tree grows fresh, new leaves.

Deciduous Tree

(has leaves)

The second group of trees are called coniferous trees. These trees have needles instead of leaves. The needles may be long or short — and sometimes they are quite sharp! Coniferous trees keep their needles all year long. The needles do not fall off the tree all at once during the fall season.

Scientists explore and examine the world around them. We can explore the world around us too, just like a real scientist! Let's examine a real tree together. As you examine the tree, think about what colors you see, any smells you notice, what the tree feels like, and what it sounds like if the wind is blowing through the tree.

Coniferous Tree

(has needles)

Activity directions:

1. Go outside and find a tree in your yard or near where you live.
2. Observe the tree together then ask your student the following questions:

   - Do you think this tree is tall or short?
   - Is the trunk wide or thin?
   - Is the bark rough or smooth? What color is the bark?
   - Do you see any leaves or needles?
   - Do you notice anything interesting about this tree?

   Bonus discussion question:

   - Do you think this tree is deciduous or coniferous? Why?

Draw a picture of the tree you saw.

Birds

week 20

Day

The Adventures of Gideon and Mr. Snuggly

Hey, friend! Since we learned about trees in our last science adventure, I thought it would be fun to learn about something that often lives in trees: birds!

Do you remember the apple tree I told you about? I once took my snack and Mr. Snuggly out to the apple tree for a picnic. As I sat on the ground, I noticed a bird fly onto a branch. It was carrying some straw in its beak. I was curious, so I watched the bird very carefully. Can you guess what the bird did with the straw? It used the straw to build a nest!

I sat very still and quiet so that I did not scare the bird away. It was fun to watch. I'd like to learn more about birds now, so let's get started!

God created many different kinds of birds; they can be fun to watch! I wonder what day of creation God created birds on. Let's read from Genesis to find out. Listen carefully as I read. Can you hear the answer?

Teacher tip: Emphasize the last sentence in the passage.

Construction paper	✓
Scissors	☐
Googly eyes	☐
Glue	☐
Craft feathers	☐
2 paper plates	☐
Stapler	☐
Crayons or markers	☐
Hole punch	☐
Yarn	☐

▶ Weekly materials list

God said, "Let the seas be filled with living things. Let birds fly above the earth across the huge space of the sky." So God created the great sea creatures. He created every kind of living thing that fills the seas and moves about in them. He created every kind of bird that flies. And God saw that it was good. God blessed them. He said, "Have little ones so that there will be many of you. Fill the water in the seas. Let there be more and more birds on the earth." There was evening, and there was morning. It was day five (Genesis 1:20–23).

Did you hear the answer? God created birds and fish on day five! Can you think of any kinds of birds you've seen in your yard, in books, or at a zoo?

Teacher tip: Allow student to answer. If they cannot think of any, you may mention penguins, ostriches, cardinals, blue jays, sparrows, parrots, or any other bird type your student may be familiar with.

There are many different kinds of birds. Some birds are quite large, like the ostrich. Other birds are small, like sparrows and hummingbirds. Some birds have bright colors like the scarlet macaw, and other birds are plain. Though there are many different birds, they all have some of the same features. Let's learn about them together!

Birds have feathers. Can you think of any jobs a bird's feathers might do?

Teacher tip: Allow student to answer.

A bird's feathers help to protect it from rain and cold weather. Birds also use their feathers to help them fly. Some feathers have plain patterns of brown, black, and white. These patterns help the bird blend in and stay safely hidden in a tree, which is called camouflage.

We're going to learn more parts of a bird later on. For today, let's color a picture of a bird. Do you think this bird has brightly colored or plain feathers? I can't wait to see how you color it!

 **Color the picture of the toucan.**

Day 2

Are you ready to learn more about birds today? Let's get started! We learned in our last adventure that birds have feathers. Birds also have a beak. The beak is on the front of the bird's face, and it often looks like a triangle. Beaks can be short and pointed or long and narrow. Birds use their beak to help them pick up food and seeds. Their beak is sharp and strong to crack through tough seeds.

Birds have wings that are covered in feathers. Most birds use their wings to fly, but not every kind of bird can fly. Penguins cannot fly, but they use their wings to swim quickly through the water!

Many kinds of birds build a nest in a tree. The nest keeps the bird's babies safe. It is a home for them. Let's create a bird nest today, as well as a bird to go in it!

materials needed
- [ ] Construction paper
- [ ] Scissors
- [ ] Googly eyes
- [ ] Glue
- [ ] Craft feathers
- [ ] 2 paper plates
- [ ] Stapler
- [ ] Crayons or markers
- [ ] Hole punch
- [ ] Yarn

Activity directions:

1. Cut one paper plate in half. Line it up on the bottom of the second paper plate to form a pouch. Staple the edges of the plates together. Give the plate pouch to your student to decorate — this will be their bird nest.

2. Use a hole punch to punch two holes out of the top of the nest. Tie yarn through the holes to create a hanger for the nest.

3. Help your student cut 1–2 circles or ovals from the construction paper — these will form the body of their bird. The cut pieces should remain small enough to fit in the paper plate nest.

4. Help your student cut small triangles — this will be the bird's beak. Glue the beak to the front of the bird's body.

5. Attach the googly eye(s) to the bird. Your student may use a crayon or marker to draw wings if they'd like.

6. Glue craft feathers to the back of the bird to create a tail. Allow to dry.

7. Once the bird(s) have dried, your student can place them in the nest.

Now, show someone your bird and tell them about the parts of a bird!

Fish

week 21

Day

The Adventures of Gideon and Mr. Snuggly

Hi, friend! I'm pretending our living room is underwater — Mr. Snuggly and I are scuba diving! We've seen some of the most colorful fish — in my imagination, anyway.

We went to the aquarium last week. They have many different fish there. I had so much fun watching them swim. I even got to feed a stingray! In our last adventure, we learned that God created birds on the fifth day of creation. But that's not all He created! God also created fish on the fifth day. Let's learn more about fish together!

During our last adventure, we learned that God created birds and fish on the fifth day of creation. Fish are living things. Fish move by swimming, they need food to eat, they grow, and they breathe. But a fish doesn't have a nose like we do, so how is a fish able to breathe? God gave fish a special design. Let's learn about it!

Take a deep breath in through your nose — can you feel the air moving through your nose?

Teacher tip: Allow student to answer.

The air around us has oxygen. When you breathe in, your body absorbs the oxygen from the air. Oxygen is a type of gas that our bodies need. When living things breathe, they breathe

- Construction paper ✓
- Glue stick ☐
- Pencil ☐
- Scissors ☐
- Googly eye ☐
- Popsicle stick ☐
- Optional: glitter glue or craft gems ☐

▶ Weekly materials list

in oxygen. There is oxygen in air and also in water. But God designed our noses to only be able to breathe in oxygen from air. People cannot breathe in water.

Fish need oxygen too, but they live in water. God designed them with a special way to be able to breathe in water. God gave fish gills to breathe. A fish's gills are found on the side of its head. To breathe, the fish opens its mouth so that water can flow through its mouth and out of its gills. As the water flows over the fish's gills, it absorbs the oxygen from the water so that the fish's body can use it. Isn't that an amazing design?

God created fish to live in the water. He designed them with fins and tails to help them swim through the water. Have you ever gone fishing and caught a fish? It may have felt very slippery in your hands! Many fish have slippery scales that also help them swim quickly through the water. God gave fish the perfect design for living in water.

This fish needs scales. Tear out small pieces of construction paper then glue them to the fish to create its scales.

Day name

Some fish are as long as a school bus, and others are even smaller than your thumb. Some fish are bright red, yellow, or orange — but others are plain so that they can hide on the ocean floor. Have you ever seen a fish in the water? What did it look like?

Teacher tip: Allow student to answer.

Fish can live in lakes, rivers, ponds, streams, and the ocean. If you're near water, you may be able to find a fish swimming there! Sometimes people can also keep fish in a fish tank in their home or at an aquarium. Does anyone you know have a fish tank?

Teacher tip: Allow student to answer. You may also discuss aquariums if you've been to one with your student.

We'll be learning about some of the other living things that live in the water soon. But first, let's create our very own fish puppet!

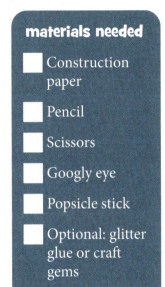

materials needed
- [ ] Construction paper
- [ ] Pencil
- [ ] Scissors
- [ ] Googly eye
- [ ] Popsicle stick
- [ ] Optional: glitter glue or craft gems

Adventures in the World Around Me ······▶ Week 21

Activity directions:

1. Use a pencil to trace your student's hand onto the construction paper.

2. If your student is able, they may cut out the traced hand. Otherwise, cut out the hand for the student.

3. With the thumb pointing up on the hand cut-out, help the student attach a googly eye to the front of the palm. They can also draw a mouth or cut one from paper and attach it to the fish.

4. Optional: The student may draw or use glitter glue/gems to decorate their fish.

5. Once the fish is dry, glue the popsicle stick to the back of it and allow it to dry. Then your student may play with their fish puppet.

Adventures in the World Around Me .... ▶ Week 21

Sharks

week 22

Day 1

The Adventures of Gideon and Mr. Snuggly

Welcome back! I was just jumping on the trampoline with Mr. Snuggly. I like to see how high I can make Mr. Snuggly bounce! It's time for another science adventure now, though. My mom said we are going to learn about sharks today. Sharks are one of my favorite creatures in the ocean, and I'm excited to learn more. I can't wait any longer. Let's get started!

God created sharks on the fifth day of creation. Sharks are large fish that live in the ocean. Sharks can move by swimming, they need food to eat, they grow, and they breathe. Sharks are living things. Sharks have gills on the sides of their body, just like smaller fish. Can you find the shark's gills in this image?

God created many different kinds of sharks to live in the ocean. Some kinds of sharks are small enough to fit in your hand, while others are far bigger than you and I! The largest shark in the ocean is called the whale shark. The whale shark can grow to be as long as a school bus.

Glue	✓
Clothespin	☐

Weekly materials list

God created the whale shark with a beautiful pattern of dots and stripes. Some kinds of sharks can be dangerous to people, but whale sharks are known as gentle giants. You may even see pictures of people swimming near a whale shark!

Whale sharks have a very large mouth on the front of their face. They swim very slowly and open their mouth wide to allow water to flow through. Water flows over their gills so that the whale shark can absorb oxygen. But that isn't the only thing the whale shark does with its mouth!

God also designed the whale shark's large mouth to be able to filter very tiny things called plankton from the water. We usually cannot see plankton with our bare eyes, but the whale shark filters plankton from the water to eat. The whale shark is one of God's amazing creations! What do you think it would be like to swim next to one in the ocean?

Color the whale shark.

name _____

Wasn't it interesting to learn about the whale shark? Let's learn about another kind of shark today: the great white shark.

The great white shark can grow to be around 20 feet long. Many grown-ups are around 5 to 6 feet tall. It would take about 4 grown-ups all standing on each other's shoulders to equal the length of a great white shark. While the great white shark isn't as long as the whale shark, it is still a large shark.

materials needed
- [ ] Glue
- [ ] Clothespin

The great white shark has a strong tail that can help it swim very quickly through the ocean. The great white shark is also called a predator. Predators eat other fish or creatures in the ocean. Predators, like the great white shark, have an important job. They help to keep the right amount of fish in the ocean, and that keeps the ocean healthy.

Blank for cutting purposes.

Scientists study fish and sharks in the ocean to learn more about how God designed them. These scientists are called marine biologists. There are still many things we can learn about fish and sharks in the ocean. What do you think it would be like to be a marine biologist who studies sharks?

Teacher tip: Allow student to answer.

In our next adventure, we're going to learn about whales and dolphins — that will be fun! But first, we have a fun shark craft. Let's make a shark puppet!

Activity directions:

1. Cut out the shark from the worksheet.
2. Glue the top of the shark to the top of the clothespin. Glue the bottom of the shark to the bottom of the clothespin.
3. Allow to dry. Once dried, your student can open and close the clothespin to open and close the shark's mouth.

Whales and Dolphins

week 23

Day

The Adventures of Gideon and Mr. Snuggly

Ahoy there, friend! Dad told me that sometimes people use the word "ahoy" to say hello when they are on a boat. Today, I'm pretending that our couch is a great big boat. Mr. Snuggly and I are searching the deep blue sea for a blue whale!

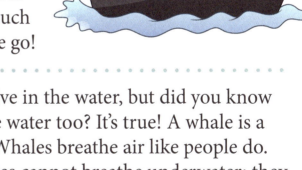

Hmm, but wait! We haven't learned about whales yet — let's learn about whales together today. Then, we can get back to our imagination adventure on our couch boat. Are you ready to learn? Here we go!

We've been learning about fish that live in the water, but did you know that other types of animals live in the water too? It's true! A whale is a large animal that lives in the ocean. Whales breathe air like people do. They do not have gills like fish. Whales cannot breathe underwater; they must swim to the surface and breathe in air.

God designed you with a nose on the front of your face. But it would be hard for a whale to breathe through a nose on the front of its face because it wouldn't be able to breathe and keep swimming. So, God gave the whale a great design! God gave the whale a blowhole on the top of its head. The whale's blowhole works like your nose — it can breathe air in and out.

Weekly materials list

- [x] Ziploc® sandwich bag
- [ ] Large bowl filled with ice water
- [ ] ½ to 1 cup butter or shortening
- [ ] Dish soap

Because the whale's blowhole is on the top of its head, the whale can swim near the surface of the water to breathe. When the blowhole is above the water, the whale can breathe in and out. This allows the whale to keep on swimming. Before the whale dives back under the water, its blowhole closes to keep water out.

The blue whale is the largest whale in the ocean. It is also the biggest animal in the world! The blue whale can grow to be as long as three school buses — that's even longer than the whale shark! The blue whale has a large mouth — but it does not have teeth like a shark. Instead, the blue whale has rows of baleen. Baleen looks a bit like the bristles on a broom.

The blue whale uses baleen to filter food out of the water. Blue whales eat krill. Krill are tiny creatures that live in the water. When it eats, the blue whale opens its mouth wide to fill it with water. Then it closes its mouth and pushes the water out through the baleen. The baleen acts like a filter. Water can pass through, but the krill cannot. The blue whale is one of God's incredible creations!

This blue whale is hungry! Trace the lines to help him find the krill.

name

We're going to continue learning about animals that live in the water today! Dolphins live in the water, but they are not fish. Dolphins breathe air through a blowhole, just like whales. Dolphins are smaller than whales.

materials needed
- ☐ Ziploc® sandwich bag
- ☐ Large bowl filled with ice water
- ☐ ½ to 1 cup butter or shortening
- ☐ Dish soap

Sometimes, dolphins live in aquariums. God created dolphins to be very smart. When dolphins live in an aquarium, they can be trained by people to perform amazing tricks and flips. Aquariums have very large tanks to hold many types of fish, dolphins, and sometimes even small whales. We can learn more about fish, dolphins, and whales at an aquarium.

Some aquariums also have beluga whales. Beluga whales live in the Arctic Ocean where the water is very cold. Do you know how the beluga is able to stay warm in cold, icy water?

Teacher tip: Allow student to answer.

God created arctic whales, like the beluga, with a special layer of fat called blubber. Blubber is under the whale's skin. The blubber helps to protect the whale from the cold and keep it warm. Blubber works kind of like how a warm jacket protects you from the cold and keeps your body warm. Hmm, I have an idea! Let's do a fun activity to see how the fatty blubber keeps the whale warm.

Activity directions:

1. Add the butter or shortening to the Ziploc® bag. Rub the outsides of the bag together to coat the inside with a layer of butter or grease.

This is fat, kind of like the blubber arctic whales have under their skin.

2. Place the bag over one of your student's hands.
3. Have your student place each hand into the bowl of ice water. Make sure the water does not enter the Ziploc® bag. See which hand can stay in the water longer.

Which hand stayed warmer in the cold water? The hand without the fat layer or the hand with the fat layer?

Animals

Day

The Adventures of Gideon and Mr. Snuggly

Hi there! I'm so excited today! I'm going to go to the zoo with my mom and big sister! What is your favorite animal? Mine is the brown bear because it looks like a big version of Mr. Snuggly. Our zoo also has a barnyard. I like to feed the goats in the barnyard. God created many different kinds of animals — would you like to learn more about animals today with me? Let's begin our adventure!

In our last few adventures, we've been learning about the living things God created. Do you remember any of the living things we've learned about?

Teacher tip: Allow student to answer.

We've learned about plants and trees, birds, fish, sharks, whales, and dolphins. We're not done yet, though! God created many different types of animals on the sixth day of creation — we can read about how God created them in Genesis 1:24–25:

God said, "Let the land produce every kind of living creature. Let there be livestock, and creatures that move along the ground, and wild animals." And that's exactly what happened. God made every kind of wild animal. He made every kind of livestock. He made every kind of creature that moves along the ground. And God saw that it was good.

Animals need to breathe air and eat food, they can grow, and they can move by themselves. Animals are living things. From the jumping rabbit, the tall giraffe, the striped tiger, and the cute puppy dog, there are many different kinds of animals on the earth. What animal is your favorite?

Teacher tip: Allow student to answer. You may also share your favorite animal.

In Genesis, we read that God created every kind of living creature. But what is a kind? A kind is the family group of the animal — like the dog family kind. There are big dogs and little dogs, and dogs with all different colors and patterns on their fur. But, no matter what the dog looks like, we can tell it is a dog.

God created many different animal kinds on the sixth day of creation. Can you think of any other animal kinds?

Teacher tip: Allow student to answer. If they cannot think of another animal kind, you may talk about cats, horses, dinosaurs, or elephants. You may also discuss the different kinds of birds and fish that God created.

If you could create an animal, what would it look like? Draw a picture of your animal below — and don't forget to give it a name!

Day Scientists who study animals are called zoologists. Zoologists can learn what an animal looks like, where it travels, what it eats, how much it sleeps, and what kinds of things it does. What do you think it would be like to be a zoologist? If you were a zoologist, what would you like to learn about an animal?

Teacher tip: Allow student to answer both questions.

As scientists study God's creation, they see some things that are similar, or the same, in some animals. For example, dogs and cats both have fur on their bodies. Can you think of anything else that both dogs and cats have?

Teacher tip: Allow student to answer. You may mention ears, eyes, paws, or tongues if your student cannot think of anything.

God created many different kinds of animals, but some animals have things that are similar to each other. Scientists organize animals into groups that have similar things. Organizing animals into groups helps us to learn more about them.

Mammals are one group of animals. Mammals are animals that feed their babies milk and have fur or hair on their bodies. Horses, dogs, cats, bears, cows, and rabbits are all part of the mammal group. Horses, dogs, cats, bears, cows, and rabbits all look different, but they each have fur or hair and feed their babies milk.

Match each mammal to its baby.

Reptiles

week 25

Day

The Adventures of Gideon and Mr. Snuggly

I've been waiting for you — I wanted to tell you what I found in our yard today! I was outside playing with Mr. Snuggly while Mom was pulling weeds from the garden. As I was playing, I noticed something moving in the grass. I called Mom so she could help me investigate. What do you think it was?

Mom and I walked closer to it very slowly, and then we saw it — it was a little turtle! The turtle had yellow stripes and red around its shell. We sat and watched it as it crawled through the grass back to our neighbor's pond. I enjoyed watching it, but it also made me curious! I want to learn more about turtles. Mom said turtles are also called reptiles. Let's learn more about them together!

As scientists study God's creation, they organize plants and animals into groups. Organizing things helps us to study and talk about different animals. In our last science adventure, we talked about the group of animals that are called mammals. Mammals feed their babies milk and have fur or hair on their bodies.

Paint	✓
Paintbrush	
Paper plate	
Glue	
Scissors	

Weekly materials list

Mammals are not the only group of animals, though! The next group of animals that scientists study are called reptiles. Reptiles have scales instead of hair or fur on their bodies. The scales may be brightly colored or quite plain. A reptile's scales are usually tough to help protect it from hot temperatures and sharp rocks.

There are many kinds of reptiles, like snakes, turtles, lizards, and crocodiles. Each kind of reptile is an interesting part of God's creation. Let's talk more about turtles today! There are many different kinds of turtles. One type of turtle you may find near a pond, creek, or river is the painted turtle. The painted turtle has yellow lines and dots along its neck and legs, and red around its shell and legs.

Painted turtles can grow to be about the size of your hand, and some are even as long as a 12-inch ruler. They like to eat plants, small fish, and insects. Some people keep painted turtles as pets. What do you think it would be like to have a pet turtle?

Teacher tip: Allow student to answer.

Activity directions:

Let's create our own turtle!

1. Turn the paper plate upside down and direct your student to paint the plate. They can use any color they'd like.

Be creative!

2. Help your student cut out the turtle head, tail, and legs from the worksheet.

3. Once the paint is dry, turn the paper plate right side up and glue the head, tail, and legs to the plate.

Page blank for cutting purposes.

name

Learning about the painted turtle during our last adventure was fun! Today, let's learn about the different ways God gave people and reptiles to keep their bodies warm.

God designed our bodies to be able to keep our temperature the same. Our bodies are able to keep themselves warm. People and mammals are called warm-blooded because our bodies can stay warm by themselves. But God designed a reptile's body differently. A reptile's body cannot keep itself the same temperature. It depends on the land or air around it to warm up or cool down.

When an animal cannot keep its body warm by itself, it is called cold-blooded. Reptiles are cold-blooded. Reptiles need something to warm up their bodies for them. When a reptile is cold, it will lay in the warm sunshine. The sun helps the reptile to warm up. When the reptile becomes too warm, it will go to the shade to cool down. It is interesting how God designed different ways for our body and a reptile's body to work, isn't it?

Activity directions:

Choose the kind of reptile you would like to pretend to be: a snake, turtle, lizard, or crocodile.

1. You can discuss how the reptile they chose would walk or slither to move.

Pretend to be the reptile you chose. You've just woken up, and it's time to crawl or slither out of your home. Your body is cold, though! Show me where you would go to warm up your body if you were a reptile.

Habitats

week 26

Day

The Adventures of Gideon and Mr. Snuggly

Oh, hello — you surprised me! I was focused on building a blanket fort for Mr. Snuggly and me to play in. I like to use my imagination to play. I'm pretending our fort is deep in the rainforest. Can you pretend with me? Be careful where you step; there are tangled tree roots all around, and the ground is wet and slippery here!

Even though I'm pretending right now, the rainforest is a real place. People, plants, mammals, birds, reptiles, and bugs live in the rainforest. My mom told me that the rainforest can also be called a habitat. Let's learn more about habitats today!

A habitat is the place a plant or animal lives in. Let's think about the painted turtle again! A painted turtle can live near a pond. Can you think of anything else we might find living at a pond?

Teacher tip: Allow student to answer.

Let's imagine a pond and some of the living things we might find there! Close your eyes and see if you can imagine the picture as I read: Next to the pond is a large rock. We see a big painted turtle resting on the rock. It is warming itself in the sun. In the

- [x] Glue stick
- [ ] Scissors

▶ Weekly materials list

middle of the pond, there's a duck. The duck is swimming through the water, and we hear its noise in the distance, "Quack, quack."

Suddenly, a fish jumps up from the water, and we hear it splash back down. As we look around the pond, we notice the trees near the pond and many plants around the outer edge. Then a dragonfly buzzes quickly past us. Wait, what is that in the distance? On the far side of the pond, there is a deer! The deer has come to the pond for a drink of water. You can open your eyes now. It was fun to imagine the pond habitat together!

A pond is a habitat where many living things all live together. Color the picture of the pond.

name _____

materials needed
☐ Glue stick
☐ Scissors

God gave the earth many different habitats, and He created living things for each type of habitat. Let's talk about some of the different habitats on the earth.

The rainforest is a hot and wet habitat. Many trees and plants grow in the rainforest. God created different kinds of monkeys, like the spider monkey and the howler monkey, that can live high in the trees of the rainforest. These monkeys have a special design for climbing and swinging between trees. God also created colorful birds like the toucan and the macaw to fly above the rainforest trees.

Another habitat is the savannah grassland. The savannah grassland is hot and dry. This habitat does not have many trees, but it does have a lot of grass! The zebra, antelope, elephant, and wildebeest all eat grass. God designed them perfectly to live in the savannah grassland! The giraffe also lives in the savannah habitat. It likes to eat leaves from the trees that grow there. God created the giraffe with a tall neck so that it can reach leaves high up on the savannah trees.

Adventures in the World Around Me ······ ▶ Week 26

The arctic habitat is cold and icy. The living things in this habitat must be able to stay warm. The polar bear lives in the arctic. God designed the polar bear with blubber under its skin, just like the beluga whale, to help keep it warm. He also gave the polar bear thick, warm fur to keep it warm on the coldest nights.

God gave the earth other habitats like the ocean, forest, and desert. He created living things that can live well in each different place. He gave each creature just what it would need to live in its habitat.

Cut out the rainforest creatures and glue them to the rainforest habitat.

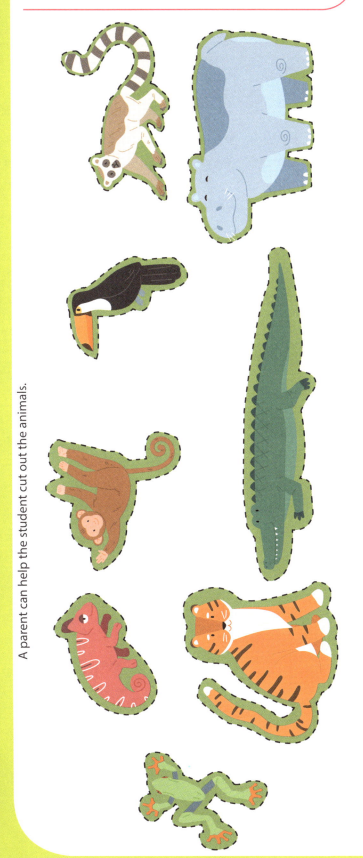

A parent can help the student cut out the animals.

Adventures in the World Around Me ······▶ Week 26

123

Page blank for cutting purposes.

Caring for the World Around Us

week 27

Day

The Adventures of Gideon and Mr. Snuggly

Hello! I'm getting ready to leave with my mom. There was a wind storm earlier this week, and the strong wind blew some garbage around our neighborhood. We're going to help our neighbors clean things up. I'm wearing my yellow rubber gloves on my hands to protect them, and I have a garbage bag to put garbage into.

The wind also knocked down a lot of branches and twigs from the trees. We're going to work together with our neighbors to clean them all up. Then tonight, we'll have a bonfire together! I hope we can make some yummy s'mores.

My mom told me this is one way we can help care for God's creation. I wonder what else we can do to care for the world around us? Hmm, let's talk about it!

God created the animals, as well as the first man and woman on the sixth day of creation. The first man's name was Adam, and the first woman's name was Eve. Let's read about how God created them in Genesis 1:26–28:

Then God said, "Let us make human beings so that they are like us. Let them rule over the fish in the seas and the birds in the sky. Let them rule over the livestock and all the wild animals. And let them rule over all the creatures that move along the ground."

So God created human beings in his own likeness.

He created them to be like himself.

He created them as male and female.

God blessed them. He said to them, "Have children so that there will be many of you. Fill the earth and bring it under your control. Rule over the fish in the seas and the birds in the sky. Rule over every living creature that moves along the ground."

God created the first two people, and He gave them a very big job: to rule over His creation. To rule means to be in charge of something and to take care of things. God gave people the job of taking care of creation.

There are many ways we can help take care of God's creation. First, we want to take good care of the things God has given us. We can take good care of the place where we live, our clothes, and our toys. Can you think of a way you can help take good care of these things?

Teacher tip: Allow student to answer.

When we take care of the little things we've been given, like our clothes and toys, it teaches us how to care for bigger things in God's creation too. We'll talk more about other ways we can help to care for God's creation in our next adventure!

Cleaning our room is one way we can care for the things God has given us. Draw a picture of your room.

name _____

God gave people the job of caring for His creation. We want to take good care of the world around us.

One way we can care for the world around us is by making sure we take care of our garbage. When garbage isn't where it belongs, it can hurt plants and animals. When we put our garbage where it belongs, we help to keep the plants and animals around us healthy.

Sometimes, we are able to care for plants inside the house or in a garden. We can make sure the plants have water and pull weeds out of the garden. Animals can be cared for too when they are pets. Do you know anyone with a pet? How do they take care of their pet?

Teacher tip: Allow student to answer both questions. Offer guidance as needed. You may mention feeding, cleaning up after, brushing, etc. If you or no one the student knows has pets, talk about how animals at a zoo are cared for.

God created many resources we can use, like food, water, and energy. We can also care for God's creation by being careful not to waste these things. We can turn off faucets when we are done washing our hands or brushing our teeth, turn off lights when we leave the room, and enjoy good food.

No matter how big or small we are, we can all help to take care of the world God made!

Optional activity:

Plan a time to help clean up your yard, a neighbor's yard, or a neighborhood park. This could involve picking up sticks or plant debris, weeding a garden, or picking up garbage. Be sure to wear rubber gloves for picking up garbage.

Oh no! This garbage was blown out of the garbage can. Trace the paths to put it back where it goes.

The Weather

week 28

Day

The Adventures of Gideon and Mr. Snuggly

Hi, friend! It's rainy at my house today.

It's been raining now for two whole days. I'm looking forward to when the sun is back out — I want to play outside with Mr. Snuggly in the sunshine.

Mom told me that our weather report says it should be warm and sunny again tomorrow. Since I need to stay inside today, I thought it would be fun to learn more about the weather and weather reports. Would you like to join me? Mom said we'll have a fun rain craft. Let's get started!

Blue construction paper	✓
Crayons	☐
Cotton balls	☐
Glue	☐
Blue paint	☐
Cotton swab	☐
Tablecloth	☐

▸ **Weekly materials list**

Have you noticed how the weather can change each day? Some days have bright, warm sunshine. Other days are windy and cool. Sometimes, it rains or snows, and a storm may even come through. There are many different kinds of weather on the earth!

Scientists study all the different kinds of weather. They use special tools that help them understand the weather. One weather tool is called a thermometer. A thermometer tells us what the temperature is so that we can tell if it is a hot, warm, cool, or cold day. Knowing the temperature helps us pick the right clothes for the weather.

Scientists who study the weather are called meteorologists. They study the patterns of the weather and use their weather tools to tell what the weather will be like ahead of time. This is called a weather report, or a forecast. The weather report can help us prepare and plan. Let's say we wanted to go to the park, but it is raining today. We could look at the weather report to see what day will be sunny and nice. Then we can plan to go to the park on that day!

Warm, sunny days are always nice — but rainy days are important too. Rain helps to clean the air and gives water to trees, plants, and other living things. Sometimes, we can even splash and play outside in the rain. That is fun too! Let's create a rainy-day picture today.

Activity directions:

1. Spread out a tablecloth to protect the table.
2. Have your student draw a picture of your home or themselves on the bottom of the construction paper.
3. Once they are done, have them glue cotton balls to the top of the construction paper to form clouds.
4. Now it's time to paint the raindrops! Let the student dip the cotton swab into the blue paint then press it to the paper to create a round raindrop. They may add as many raindrops as they'd like. Allow the project to dry.

name _____

Meteorologists are scientists who study the weather. Meteorologists have an important job; they can tell us when sunny days are coming and even when a storm will come through.

Thunderstorms are a type of stormy weather. During thunderstorms, it can rain very hard. The rumbly thunder makes a loud noise, and the bright lightning flashes through the sky. Just like rainy days, thunderstorms help to clean the air. Thunderstorms also help to keep the soil healthy so that plants and trees can grow well.

Stormy weather can be loud, and it can make us feel afraid sometimes. Did you know that even King David in the Bible felt afraid sometimes? King David knew what to do when he felt afraid, though; he put his trust in God. In Psalm 56:3, he wrote,

When I'm afraid, I put my trust in you.

No matter what the weather is like — sunny, windy, rainy, snowy, or stormy — we can put our trust in God, too. What is your favorite kind of weather?

Teacher tip: Allow student to answer.

Do you remember how we can use our eyes as science tools to observe what is around us? Let's use our eyes today to observe the weather outside. Then we can complete our worksheet.

Circle the correct answer.

Today, it is:

Hot   Warm   Cool   Cold

The weather is:

Is it windy?

Yes   No

Draw a picture of what it looks like outside today.

Spring & Summer

week 29

Day

The Adventures of Gideon and Mr. Snuggly

It's time for another science adventure together, friend! I've been thinking about the four seasons lately. The four seasons are spring, summer, fall, and winter. There are so many things we can enjoy during each season! Last spring, my family went on a hike. I carried Mr. Snuggly the whole way! We found a beautiful waterfall at the end of the hike, and we ate our lunch there.

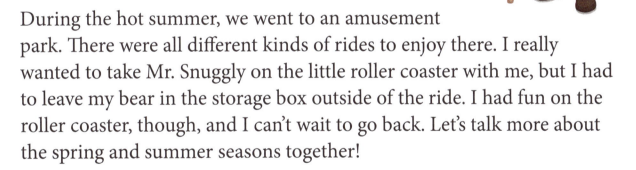

During the hot summer, we went to an amusement park. There were all different kinds of rides to enjoy there. I really wanted to take Mr. Snuggly on the little roller coaster with me, but I had to leave my bear in the storage box outside of the ride. I had fun on the roller coaster, though, and I can't wait to go back. Let's talk more about the spring and summer seasons together!

Weekly materials list

- Paper plate ✓
- Yellow or orange paint ☐
- Paintbrush ☐
- Scissors ☐
- Yellow or orange construction paper ☐
- Tablecloth ☐

God gave the earth four seasons. Each season helps the earth in different ways and gives us different things to enjoy. Let's talk about the spring season first!

In the spring, the weather becomes warmer. We enjoy the warm, spring sunshine after the cold winter. It may rain often during the spring — these rain showers are important for the plants.

Plants need plenty of water to begin growing in the spring. Spring rain showers give water to the trees, plants, flowers, grass, and other living things.

The leaves begin to grow again on the trees in the springtime. Beautiful flowers grow quickly. In some places, the flowers begin to grow before the snow has even fully melted! Fruit trees grow flowers that smell nice. They make the spring air smell fresh and sweet.

Flowers have pollen and nectar. Nectar is like a sweet drink that bees, butterflies, and insects love. Pollen is like a sticky powder. During the spring, we may hear the hum of buzzing bees and insects all around the pretty flowers. The bees and insects are eating nectar! While they eat, their legs and body get covered in the sticky pollen.

When the bees and insects fly to the next flower to eat more nectar, they leave some pollen behind and pick up new pollen on their legs. This is called pollination. Pollination helps trees and plants to make fruits and vegetables. Bees and insects are an important part of God's creation!

Help the bee fly to the flower by tracing the line.

name

materials needed
- [ ] Paper plate
- [ ] Yellow or orange paint
- [ ] Paintbrush
- [ ] Scissors
- [ ] Yellow or orange construction paper
- [ ] Tablecloth

It was fun to learn a little more about the spring season; now let's talk about summer! During the summer season, it can be quite hot outside. We usually don't get as much rain, and the sun shines strong and bright.

The trees have all of their leaves and are full and green during the summer. Many plants grow fruits and vegetables during the summer that we can enjoy eating. What is your favorite fruit or vegetable?

Teacher tip: Allow student to answer.

During hot summer days, we can enjoy swimming or playing in a sprinkler. Many families enjoy picnics, barbecues, or traveling to different places. When we play outside during the summer, it is important to make sure we drink plenty of water. Our bodies need water to stay healthy, especially when it is hot outside. We can also be careful to protect our skin and eyes from the strong sunlight. We can wear sunglasses, hats, and sunscreen.

The sun gives us plenty of light and heat during the summer. Let's create a summer sun craft today!

Activity directions:

1. Spread a tablecloth to protect the table.

2. Place the paper plate upside down on the table. Have your student paint the plate yellow or orange.

3. As the plate dries, help your student cut strips of paper from the construction paper. The strips should be about 1–2 inches wide and about 5–6 inches long.

4. Once the plate is dry, flip it right-side up.

5. Let the student glue the strips of construction paper to the edge of the plate to create sun rays. Allow to dry.

Fall & Winter

week 30

Day

The Adventures of Gideon and Mr. Snuggly

I had fun talking about the spring and summer seasons with you! It's time to explore the fall and winter seasons now. These seasons also have so many things we can enjoy! During the fall, my mom takes me to the pumpkin patch. We get to see many big, orange pumpkins. We also go on a hayride! Mr. Snuggly gets all covered in straw during the hayride.

When it is wintertime, my big sister takes me sledding. I like to take Mr. Snuggly sledding with me. One time, my sled went so fast that Mr. Snuggly flew right off! Mr. Snuggly landed in the snow. When I picked him up, it left a bear-print in the snow! I made a snow angel right next to Mr. Snuggly's bear-print, and Mom took a picture. Let's talk more about the fall and winter seasons!

The fall season comes after summer. During the fall, the weather begins to get cooler outside. We may need to wear sweaters or jackets to help us stay warm when we play outside.

As the weather becomes cooler, the plants begin to prepare for winter. Fruits and vegetables that have grown during the summer are now ready

Weekly materials list

- [x] White, blue, black, and orange construction paper
- [ ] Pencil
- [ ] Yarn
- [ ] Scissors
- [ ] Glue stick
- [ ] Googly eyes
- [ ] Optional: cotton balls or white glitter glue

to be harvested. Some plants wither and turn brown — but below the dirt, their roots will stay alive, waiting for the warm spring weather to return. When it does, the plants will begin to grow again.

The trees also prepare for winter during the fall. A tree's leaves need sunshine, and there won't be enough sunshine for them during the winter. So, the tree will let its leaves fall off to prepare for winter. The leaves will turn brown, yellow, orange, or red before they fall off the tree. Some families rake up large piles of fallen leaves to play in. The fall leaf colors can be very beautiful!

These leaves have fallen from the trees. Color them red, orange, yellow, and brown.

name _____

materials needed
- [ ] White, blue, black, and orange construction paper
- [ ] Pencil
- [ ] Yarn
- [ ] Scissors
- [ ] Glue stick
- [ ] Googly eyes
- [ ] Optional: cotton balls or white glitter glue

Let's talk about the winter season now! The winter is a time of rest. The trees and plants rest as they wait for the warm spring weather to return. Some types of animals, like bears, groundhogs, and skunks, hibernate through the winter. When an animal hibernates, it goes into a deep sleep for days, weeks, or even months! Can you imagine what it would be like to be asleep for a month?

Teacher tip: Allow student to answer.

Plants and trees are also resting during the winter. When trees and plants are resting, we say they are dormant. On the outside, it may look like a tree or plant isn't alive anymore. But God designed them to stay dormant through the winter to protect themselves from the cold. Once the weather is warm again, the plants and trees will begin to grow once more.

It can be very cold outside during the winter. We may need heavy coats, mittens, and hats to help keep us warm when we play outside. In some places of the world, snow falls during the winter. Some areas receive a lot of snow! It can be fun to play in the snow and make snowmen, snow angels, and go sledding. Let's make a paper snowman together today!

Adventures in the World Around Me .... ▸ Week 30

Activity directions:

Allow the student to do the cutting and gluing for this project as they are able. The teacher may assist or do it for them.

1. Draw 3 circles on the white paper. If your student is able, have them cut out the circles. If not, you may cut them out.

2. Glue the circles to the blue piece of paper to create the snowman's body.

3. Give 2 googly eyes to your student to place on the snowman's head.

4. Draw a small triangle on the orange paper to form the snowman's nose and cut it out. Glue the triangle nose to the snowman.

5. Cut a square and rectangle from the black construction paper to create a hat for the snowman. Glue the pieces to the snowman's head.

6. Cut a small piece of yarn to form the snowman's scarf. Glue the scarf to the snowman.

7. Have your student draw the snowman's arms and smile.

8. Optional: Your student may glue cotton balls or use glitter glue along the bottom of the construction paper to create a snowy ground.

Daytime

week 31

Day

The Adventures of Gideon and Mr. Snuggly

Hello! I'm glad you're here. I've been waiting to tell you about my morning today. I woke up really early. My dad was still getting ready for work. Once he was ready, I asked if we could sit outside on the front porch and listen to the birds singing for a little while. He said yes, so I grabbed Mr. Snuggly and we went outside together.

We watched the sunrise while the birds were singing. It was a beautiful sunrise, and I'm glad I got to see it with my dad. The sunrise also gave me an idea! I'd like to learn more about the sun and daytime — let's get started!

God created the daytime and the nighttime. Let's talk about the daytime first! During the day, we can work, play, learn, eat, and have fun together. God created the sun to give us light during the day while we do all these things. Do you know what day God created the sun on? Let's read from Genesis 1:14–19 to find out! Listen carefully as I read. Can you hear the answer?

Teacher tip: Emphasize the last sentence.

Globe or ball	✓
Flashlight	☐
Dark room	☐

▶ **Weekly materials list**

Adventures in the World Around Me ········▶ Week 31

God said, "Let there be lights in the huge space of the sky. Let them separate the day from the night. Let the lights set the times for the holy celebrations and the days and the years. Let them be lights in the huge space of the sky to give light on the earth." And that's exactly what happened. God made two great lights. He made the larger light to rule over the day and the smaller light to rule over the night. He also made the stars. God put the lights in the huge space of the sky to give light on the earth. He put them there to rule over the day and the night. He put them there to separate light from darkness. God saw that it was good. There was evening, and there was morning. It was day four (Genesis 1:14–19).

The larger light that God made is the sun, and the smaller light is the moon — did you hear when God created them?

Teacher tip: Allow student to answer.

God created them on day four! The sun is a star. We'll talk more about stars soon. But for now, stars burn hot, and they give light and heat. The sun burns hot, and it gives the earth the perfect amount of light and heat. Without the sun, the earth would be too cold and dark for us to live on. I'm glad God created the sun perfectly, aren't you?

The sun gives us light so that we can do things during the day. What is your favorite thing to do during the daytime? Draw a picture of you doing your favorite thing below.

name

Teacher tip: This lesson will cover the earth's orbit, which is an abstract concept for young students. This lesson is intended to be an introduction to the topic, and the student's full understanding is not required. The activity in week 32 will further build on this topic.

materials needed
- [ ] Globe or ball
- [ ] Flashlight
- [ ] Dark room

God created the sun to give us light and heat. The sun is always there, but we cannot always see it. Do you wonder why? We're going to learn why today!

The earth and the sun are shaped like balls. The sun is far, far bigger than the earth, and it has a lot of gravity. The earth has gravity too — gravity is what keeps your feet on the ground and pulls you back down when you jump. Can you jump for me?

Teacher tip: Allow student to jump. Reinforce that gravity pulled them back down.

Just like the earth's gravity pulls on you to keep you on the ground, the sun's gravity also pulls on the earth to keep it in the right place. The sun's gravity pulls on the earth and causes it to travel all the way around the sun. We call this an orbit. It takes the earth one year to travel all the way around the sun in its orbit. But that's not all!

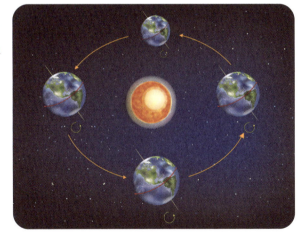

While the earth is traveling in a circle around the sun, it is also spinning around in a circle. We cannot feel it move, but the earth spins around one time each day. As it spins, half of the earth faces the sun. If we live on the half of the earth that is facing the sun, we can see the sun, and it will be daytime! Half of the earth is hidden from the sun, though. It will be nighttime on that side. Would you like to see how this works?

Activity directions:

1. Take the supplies and your student into a dark room.
2. Hold the globe or ball on one side of the room. Have the student shine the flashlight on the globe from the other side of the room.

The light is shining on that side of the globe — it would be daytime on that side. But on the other side, it is dark — it is nighttime there.

3. Trade places with your student so that they can observe both the light and dark side of the globe.
4. Have your student spin the globe or ball and observe how half is always in the light, while half is in the dark — just like the earth.

Nighttime

Day

The Adventures of Gideon and Mr. Snuggly

Hi there! We camped in our backyard last night; it was such a fun time! Dad built a campfire, and we made s'mores. Mom and Dad told us stories about when they were kids — some of their stories were funny!

Once the fire started to go out, we looked at the moon so high up in the sky. The moon was bright and beautiful. Then we counted as many stars as we could before going into the tent to sleep. I want to learn more about the moon and stars in our science adventure — would you like to join me? Let's go learn!

- ✓ Black construction paper
- ☐ Pencil
- ☐ Gray paint
- ☐ Paper plate
- ☐ Tinfoil
- ☐ White or silver glitter glue
- ☐ Tablecloth
- ☐ Scissors
- ☐ Brad fasteners

▶ Weekly materials list

At the end of the day, we watch the sunset fade away, and the nighttime begins. During the night, the sun is shining on the other side of the earth, but it is dark on our side. God created the sun, moon, and stars on the fourth day of creation. The moon and stars give us a gentle light during the nighttime. Let's talk about them!

Just like the earth orbits around the sun, the moon also orbits around the earth. We'll talk more about that next time! As the moon orbits, though, it reflects light from the sun back to earth. This gives the moon its soft glow in the night sky.

God filled the sky with many stars — more stars than we can count! The sun is the closest star to the earth — other stars are much, much farther away. That is why the stars in the night sky look so small. They are very, very far away from earth. Stars burn gases and they are extremely hot.

God gave us the night as a time to rest our bodies. Sleep is important for our bodies, and it is easier to sleep when it is dark. Aren't you glad God gave us the nighttime and gentle light from the moon and stars? Let's create a nighttime picture!

Activity directions:

1. Spread out the tablecloth.
2. Help your student draw a large circle on the paper. This will be the outline for the moon.
3. Put the gray paint on a paper plate and crumple tin-foil into a small ball.
4. Show your student how to dip the tinfoil ball into the paint and then "stamp" it onto the moon outline. Have your student paint the moon this way.
5. Once the moon has dried, it's time to add some stars! Your student may add dots of white or silver glitter glue to create the stars. They may add as many as they'd like. Allow to dry.

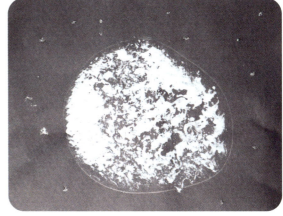

Day

name

Teacher tip: This lesson is intended to be a further introduction to the concept of orbits, and the student's full understanding is not required.

materials needed
- [ ] Scissors
- [ ] Brad fasteners

Just like the sun, the earth also has gravity. The earth's gravity keeps our feet on the ground. The earth's gravity also pulls on the moon and causes it to travel around the earth — just like the sun pulls on the earth. Remember, this is called an orbit. The moon travels around the earth in an orbit, and the earth travels around the sun in an orbit. Isn't that neat?

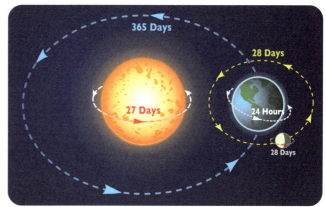

I have an idea for today. Let's create a model of the earth and the moon's orbits so that we can see what they are like. Ready to get started?

Activity directions:

1. Help your student cut out the pieces from the worksheet.
2. Hold the sun and place the earth's long strip of paper underneath. Push a brad fastener through the middle of the sun and into the strip of paper to fasten the earth and the sun together.
3. Place the moon's strip of paper underneath the middle of the earth. Push a brad fastener through the middle of the earth to fasten the layers together.
4. Slowly and carefully rotate the moon around the earth to loosen up the paper around the fastener. Repeat with the sun. Your student may then rotate each to see how orbits work.

The sun's gravity causes the earth to travel around the sun in an orbit. The earth's gravity causes the moon to travel around the earth in an orbit.

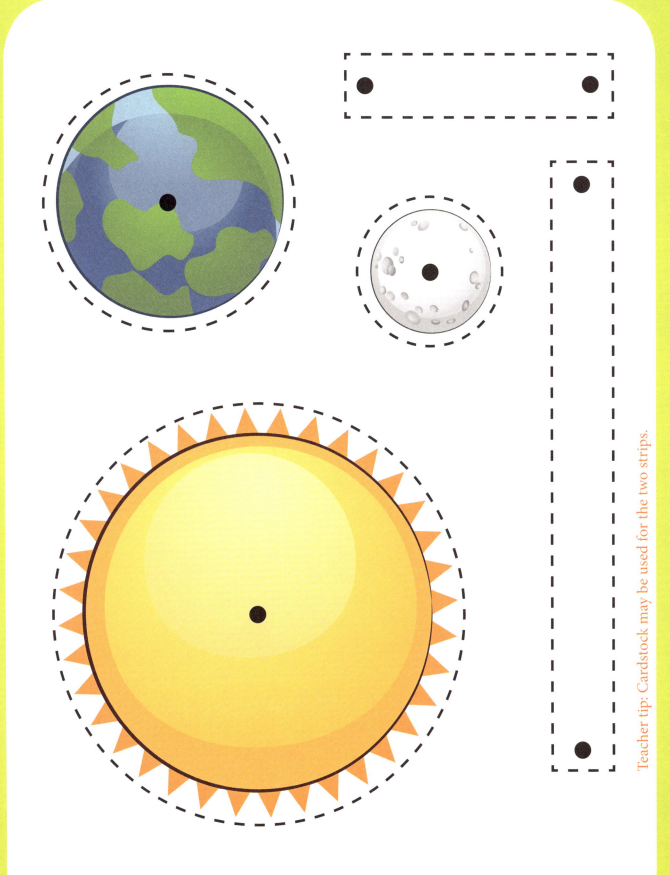

Teacher tip: Cardstock may be used for the two strips.

Adventures in the World Around Me ▸ Week 32

149

Page blank for cutting purposes.

Rocks & Minerals

week 33

Day

The Adventures of Gideon and Mr. Snuggly

Hi, friend! This morning, I went to a museum with my mom and sister. We saw many interesting things, and it was a lot of fun. Before we left, we stopped at the museum's gift shop. The gift shop had beautiful rocks that we could buy. I filled a little pouch with my favorite rocks, and Mom bought them for me.

My little pouch of rocks gave me an idea for our next science adventure! I'd like to learn more about rocks and minerals. Would you like to join me? Let's get started!

Scientists explore, observe, and organize things in God's creation. Organizing things into groups helps us to talk about and learn more about them.

Though there are many different kinds of rocks on the earth, scientists can organize them into three groups, called sedimentary, igneous, and metamorphic rocks. Let's talk about these groups!

- A pumice stone ✓
- Magnifying glass ☐
- Salt ☐

▶ **Weekly materials list**

Sedimentary rocks are made by layers of very small pieces of broken rocks, dirt, and sand. Sandstone is a type of sedimentary rock. If you look very closely at sandstone, you may see tiny pieces of sand, dirt, and broken rocks. These tiny pieces are called grains.

You may also see layers in sedimentary rock. These layers are formed by water. Water carries the grains of sand, dirt, and broken rocks. Eventually, the grains fall to the bottom of the water and begin to form the layers of the rock. Once the rock is hardened, we can see the layers of rock, sand, and dirt. Sedimentary rocks are special because they often have fossils — we're going to learn about fossils soon!

Igneous rocks are formed from volcanoes. On the inside, volcanoes are very hot, and they are filled with rock that has melted. When a volcano erupts, this melted rock comes to the top of the volcano as hot lava. The lava won't stay hot for long outside of the volcano, though. As the lava cools, igneous rocks are formed.

Pumice is one type of igneous rock. Pumice is full of holes because air was trapped inside the lava as it cooled. Once the pumice is cooled, the air escapes, and the holes are left behind. Pumice is often used in blocks or ground up and put in soaps to help keep our skin clean and smooth.

The third type of rocks are called metamorphic rocks. Metamorphic is a big word that means change. Metamorphic rocks used to be sedimentary or igneous rocks, but they were changed by heat and pressure. Sandstone changes to quartzite when there is heat and pressure. Quartzite is very strong and can be used to create kitchen countertops and even flooring.

Rocks can be very useful! Let's look at some pumice together now.

Activity directions:

Give your student the pumice stone and a magnifying glass. Have them examine the stone.

- How does this rock feel?
- Is it light or heavy?
- What color is it?
- Do you see the holes in this rock? Do you remember how those holes were formed?

name

Today, let's learn about minerals! Minerals were created by God. We find them all over the earth. There is one type of mineral we use often in the kitchen and dining room. Do you have any idea what it might be?

materials needed
☐ Salt

Teacher tip: Allow student to answer. Then sprinkle salt on the table or into your student's hand.

Salt is a mineral! Salt can be found in the oceans and underground. Salt is very useful. Our bodies need very small amounts of salt in order to stay healthy. We often use salt when we cook our food because salt gives it a good flavor.

Teacher tip: If you have diamond jewelry, allow your student to examine it.

Diamonds are another kind of mineral. Diamonds are found deep within the earth. They must be cut and polished to make beautiful jewelry. But that isn't all diamonds are used for! Diamonds are extremely hard and strong. Diamonds can be used in machines or to help cut things. Some kinds of saw blades use diamonds so that they can cut through very hard materials.

God gave us many different kinds of minerals on the earth. Amethyst has a beautiful purple color and can be used to make jewelry. Color the amethyst below.

Fossils

> week 34

Day

The Adventures of Gideon and Mr. Snuggly

Hey there! You won't believe what I found while I was playing outside today! I noticed a strange-looking rock while I was driving Mr. Snuggly around in my toy dump truck. I was curious, so I picked up the rock and took it over to my mom. When my mom looked at it, she realized that my strange-looking rock was really the fossil of a stick!

I can't wait to show Dad my fossil stick when he gets home tonight. Mom said she would teach me all about fossils in the meantime. Would you like to join me? Let's get started!

We have an exciting science adventure ahead of us today! But before we get started, we need to learn a new word. Our new word for today is preserve. Preserve means to keep something safe or protected.

Hmm, let's think of a way we could preserve something — oh, I have an idea! After we play with Play-Doh®, we put it back into the container. The container preserves the Play-Doh® so that it stays soft for us to play with. Without the container, the Play-Doh® would dry out and we wouldn't be able to create things with it anymore.

Now, feel your wrist or elbow. Do you feel the hard parts underneath your skin? Those are your bones! Bones help you to stand and move. God created people and many kinds of animals and fish with bones.

- [✓] Plate
- [ ] Chocolate chip cookie
- [ ] Toothpick or chopstick
- [ ] Paintbrush

▶ **Weekly materials list**

Let's get back to learning about fossils now. A fossil is part of a plant, fish, or animal that has been preserved — which means kept safe and protected — in rock. Fossils usually show the bones or hard parts of a plant, fish, or animal. But sometimes, we find fossils of leaves or even footprints!

So, how are fossils formed? Let's imagine Gideon's twig fossil from the story. When a twig falls to the ground from a tree, it will break apart over time. The twig will break apart into little bits and pieces until eventually it is just dirt, and no one ever knows it was there!

Fossils are different, though. If a plant, fish, or animal — or our twig — is buried very quickly by dirt and water, it can become a fossil. Do you remember what we learned about sedimentary rock? Sedimentary rocks are made of pieces of dirt, rock, and sand that were carried by water. Fossils also need pieces of dirt, rock, sand, and water to form. Sedimentary rock is the perfect place for fossils to form.

Once the hard parts, like wood, bones, or teeth, are buried, water and minerals turn the hard parts into rock. The rock preserves the shape of the plant, sea creature, or animal's bones and teeth so that we can see what it looked like when it was living. We find fossils of trees, plants, insects, fish, and other sea creatures, dinosaurs, animals, and more!

A scientist who studies fossils is called a paleontologist. Paleontologists find and excavate fossils. Excavate is a big word that means to carefully dig a fossil out from the rock around it. Let's pretend to be a paleontologist today!

Activity directions:

1. Place the chocolate chip cookie on the plate.
2. Give your student the toothpick or chopstick and the paintbrush.

Let's pretend that this cookie is a rock and that the chocolate chips are fossils inside the rock. You can use the toothpick to carefully scrape away the cookie from around the chocolate chip. You can use the paintbrush to brush away the cookie crumbs. Can you excavate the chocolate chips just like a paleontologist excavates fossils?

Have fun! See how many chocolate chips you can excavate from the cookie.

name

Fossils are the hard parts of a plant, sea creature, or animal that have been preserved, or kept safe, for us to see in rock. When we find a fossil, we are able to see part of something that lived hundreds or thousands of years ago. When we find the fossil of an animal, we can see the size and shape of its teeth. We can see how tall it was and what its bones looked like. We can imagine what it might have looked like when it was alive.

Fossils show us evidence of creatures that lived in the past. Sometimes, we find fossils of creatures that we still see today. Paleontologists find fossils of dogs and cats. These fossils look similar to dogs and cats that are living today because God created the dog and cat kinds.

Sometimes, though, we find fossils of creatures that no longer exist today — like the dinosaurs. We do not see living dinosaurs today, like we see living cats and dogs. When an animal kind is no longer living on the earth, we say they are extinct. Extinct animals, like the dinosaurs, were created by God. We'll talk more about dinosaurs next time!

Match each fossil to the type of animal it was.

Dinosaurs

week 35

Day

The Adventures of Gideon and Mr. Snuggly

Rawr! Oh, I mean hello, friend! I'm pretending that Mr. Snuggly and I are dinosaurs today. What kind of dinosaur do you think I am pretending to be? I'm pretending to be my favorite dinosaur, the huge brachiosaurus!

The brachiosaurus had four long legs, along with a long tail and a long neck. Dad told me that the brachiosaurus could grow to be as long as the blue whale! Can you imagine what it might have been like to see one of these creatures outside of your house? Hey, that gives me an idea — let's talk about dinosaurs today!

Dinosaurs were amazing creatures that God created on the sixth day of creation. God created all the land animals on the sixth day of creation, as well as the first two people on the earth! Their names were Adam and Eve. God gave Adam the job of naming all the living creatures. Adam would have named the dinosaurs that God created. What do you think that would have been like?

Teacher tip: Allow student to answer.

We read in the Bible that God's original creation was perfect. All living things — including lions, bears, and even dinosaurs — were friendly.

Play-Doh® ✓

Weekly materials list

They did not hurt each other. The Bible tells us that God created all living things to eat fruits and vegetables. Even the tyrannosaurus rex with its sharp, long teeth would have used them to chomp on yummy fruits and vegetables!

But it didn't stay that way for long. God gave Adam and Eve directions, but they chose not to obey God's directions. When we do not obey God's directions, it is called sin. Sin broke God's creation — things could no longer be perfect. After sin, sad things began to happen, and some animals like lions, bears, and dinosaurs were no longer friendly as God had created them to be.

Sin is the reason sad things happen in God's creation. But the saddest of all is that sin separates us from God. Thankfully, that isn't the end of the story, though! We're going to talk about the rest of the story soon.

Color this picture of the triceratops. What would you have named it?

name

God created many different kinds of dinosaurs. Some kinds were much smaller than you, while others were very tall and mighty creatures. But we don't see dinosaurs alive today — so how do we know about them? We know about dinosaurs through fossils!

materials needed
☐ Play-Doh®

The Bible tells us about a Flood that covered the whole world in water. God warned a man named Noah that the Flood was coming. God told Noah to build a large boat called an ark. The Ark would protect Noah and his family, as well as two of each kind of animal and bird. Noah followed God and did everything God had told him to do.

Then, just as God said it would, the Flood covered the earth. Though some dinosaurs would have been safe inside Noah's Ark, dinosaurs that were not inside the Ark died in the Flood. These dinosaurs were quickly covered up in sand, dirt, rocks, and water. When that happens, a fossil can be created.

Many dinosaurs were fossilized because of the great Flood. After the Flood, Noah and his family, along with all the animals, dinosaurs, and birds, left the Ark. But the world was different now, and it was much harder for some creatures, like the dinosaurs, to survive. Over time, the very last one of some creatures, like the dinosaurs, died. Remember, when an animal kind is no longer living on the earth, we say they are extinct.

Though dinosaurs are extinct now, paleontologists find their fossils. Paleontologists carefully dig up the fossils so that we can learn about what dinosaurs looked like. Sometimes, we can see the fossils of a dinosaur, like an allosaurus, at a museum. The allosaurus stood on two legs and was much taller than a person. It had two small arms and a big head with sharp teeth.

The mighty allosaurus, like every kind of dinosaur, was created by God. Dinosaur fossils show us evidence that these amazing creatures once lived, and they remind us that sin caused sad things to happen in God's creation.

If you could create a dinosaur, what would it be like? Where would it live and what would it eat? Create your own kind of dinosaur using Play-Doh®. You can also draw your dinosaur below — and don't forget to give it a name!

My dinosaur's name

Teacher tip: You can write the name of the student's dinosaur and allow them to trace it.

Conclusion

week 36

Day

The Adventures of Gideon and Mr. Snuggly

Can you believe we're already to the end of our science adventures for now? I've had so much fun exploring the world God made with you! Do you remember the things we've explored together this year? We've learned about how we can use our five senses to explore God's creation and how to take good care of ourselves. We talked about light and shadows, colors, size, shape, water, heat, and all kinds of living things.

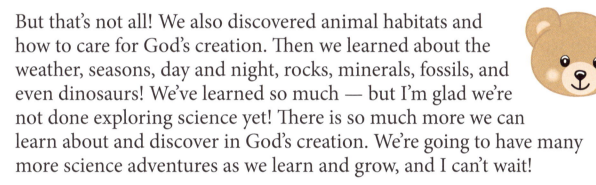

But that's not all! We also discovered animal habitats and how to care for God's creation. Then we learned about the weather, seasons, day and night, rocks, minerals, fossils, and even dinosaurs! We've learned so much — but I'm glad we're not done exploring science yet! There is so much more we can learn about and discover in God's creation. We're going to have many more science adventures as we learn and grow, and I can't wait!

I've had so much fun with you this year exploring the world God created through science! What was your favorite adventure?

Teacher tip: Allow student to answer.

There are many things we can explore in God's creation. We can learn so much more about rocks and land, fossils, ocean life, weather, animals, birds, insects, air, water, plants, and more! Sometimes when we explore science, though, we see sad things in God's creation. People or animals may be hurt or become sick, and that makes us sad.

When we see sad things in creation, it reminds us that sin broke creation. It is no longer perfect the way God created it to be at the beginning. God knows what is best for us, and He gives us directions in the Bible. When we do not follow God's directions, it is sin. Sin hurts us and other people. Sin also separates us from God.

The Bible tells us that sin has a very high price that must be paid. God sent His Son, Jesus, to pay the price for our sin for us. The price of sin is death; Jesus died to pay the price for our sin so that we can be close to God. Then Jesus rose from the dead — He's alive! Jesus beat sin and death so that we can be close to God forever. In the Bible, John 3:16 (NIV) says:

For God so loved the world that he gave his one and only Son, that whoever believes in him shall not perish but have eternal life.

God loves the world. He loves you and me and all people. I'm so glad God loves us so much that He sent Jesus to pay the price for our sin, aren't you? Because Jesus paid the price, we can have a relationship with God when we ask Jesus to forgive our sins and put our trust in Him. The Bible also tells us that someday God will create a new heavens and a new earth. Things will be perfect once more, and we will spend all of forever together with God if we have put our trust in Him.

The Bible teaches us about God and about how we can follow Him. Color the picture.

name _____

When we study science, we learn more about how God created the world. We also get to discover God's amazing designs in creation and learn more about Him! There are many different parts of science that we can explore. Each part of science is called a branch, or field, of science.

One branch of science is called geology. Scientists who study geology are called geologists. Geologists study rocks and dirt. Another branch of science is called biology. Scientists who study biology are called biologists. Biologists learn about living things.

Paleontology, zoology, and marine biology are just a few other branches of science that we've also talked about. There are many different branches of science that we can explore God's creation through. What part of God's creation would you like to learn more about next?

Teacher tip: Allow student to answer.

It is fun to explore God's creation through science — and I can't wait to have many more science adventures with you. In the meantime, congratulations! You've completed our science adventure as we've explored the world around us. Do you know what that means? You're a certified junior science explorer!

Blank for certificate.